P9-CEF-588

Classifying Living Things

Theme: Systems

THINK LIKE A SCIENTIST

THINK
LIKE A SCIENTIST

SCHOOL'S OUT

Fish, such as this school of brightly colored fairy basslets, are just one of the many kinds of living things in the world. Scientists who study living things observe their traits, or characteristics. These traits are used by scientists to classify living things. And by classifying living things, scientists can study them more easily and can learn how living things meet their basic needs.

THINK LIKE A SCIENTIST

Questioning In this unit you'll study fish and many other living things. You'll investigate questions such as these:

- How Can Living Things Be Classified?
- How Do Living Things Meet Their Needs?

Observing, Testing, Hypothesizing In the Activity "Animals Are Different," you'll make observations about the traits of three different animals. You'll also infer how body parts help each animal survive.

Researching In the Resource "Variety of Life on Earth," you'll gather more information about how animals and other living things are classified.

Drawing Conclusions After you've completed your investigations, you'll draw conclusions about what you've learned—and get new ideas.

CHAPTER 1

ALL KINDS OF LIVING THINGS

What's your favorite plant or animal? Are there other plants or animals that are similar to it? In this chapter you'll learn about many kinds of living things. As you explore, think about ways that living things are similar and different.

PEOPLE USING SCIENCE

Field Biologist You may have seen a macaw (mə kô′) at the zoo, a pet store, or in someone's home. These large parrots live in the tropical rain forests of South America. Macaws nest in trees more than 31 m (100 ft) off the ground. Eduardo Nycander is a field biologist. He studies wild macaws at a research station in the Amazon forest of Peru. He discovered that macaws have a hard time finding hollow tree trunks that can serve as suitable places to build nests. Eduardo Nycander now works at providing macaws with plastic nests. The nests are hollow tubes about 35.6 cm (14 in.) wide and 2.4 m (8 ft) long. Nycander climbs high above the ground and straps the nests to the tree trunks. The birds love them! The nests look like hollow tree trunks. What would you ask Eduardo Nycander about his work?

◀ Field biologist Eduardo Nycander checks on a macaw chick 31 m (100 ft) above the ground.

HOW CAN LIVING THINGS BE CLASSIFIED?

Suppose you made a list of all the living things that you could think of. How would you classify them to make it easy to study them? Find out in this investigation how scientists classify living things.

Activity

Animals Are Different

Which animal is a cat more like—a catfish or a dog? How would you decide? In this activity you'll make observations that could be used to classify animals.

MATERIALS
- hand lens
- 3 animals for observation
- *Science Notebook*

SAFETY /////
Do not touch the animals unless you have your teacher's permission.

Procedure

1. Your teacher will give your group three different animals to observe. As you **observe** the animals, look for ways that they are alike and ways that they are different.

Step 1

2. In your *Science Notebook*, **make a chart** like the one shown below. Add as many different traits, or characteristics, as you can think of. **Record** your observations under the column for each animal.

Traits	Animal 1	Animal 2	Animal 3
How It Moves			
Type of Body Covering			
Number of Legs/Description			
Number of Eyes			
Number of Ears			
Where It Might Live			

3. **Record** the ways you think these living things are alike and the ways they are different.

4. You may want to use a hand lens to **observe** some animals more closely. **Record** any further observations you make. **Infer** where each animal might live and **record** your inference.

 See **SCIENCE** *and* **MATH TOOLBOX** page H2 *if you need to review **Using a Hand Lens**.*

Analyze and Conclude

1. Are there any traits that all the animals share? If so, what are they?

2. **Infer** how each animal's body parts help it survive.

3. **Infer** which of the animals might have a backbone. Give reasons for your inferences.

Variety of Life on Earth

> **Reading Focus** Into what large groups can organisms be classified?

How many kinds of living things could there be on Earth—hundreds? thousands? The answer is millions! Millions of kinds of **organisms** (ôr′gə niz əmz), or living things, exist on Earth.

Living things can be found in oceans, forests, deserts, mountains, soil, air—almost everywhere on Earth. And incredibly, many scientists classify, or group, all organisms into just five large groups, called kingdoms.

Organisms placed in the same kingdom share certain traits, or characteristics. Scientists use the different traits of living things to classify them. The number of cells, the basic units that make up all organisms, is just one trait used to classify living things. Other traits include life processes, such as how an organism gets food or reproduces. Study the table and the pictures on the next page to see the general traits shared by living things in each kingdom.

How many kinds of living things can you find in this picture? ▼

Kingdoms of Living Things

Kingdom	Examples	Traits
Animal	horse, dog, bird, fish, spider, worm, starfish, coral	• many-celled • most have structures for moving from place to place • feed on other organisms • reproduce by eggs or live birth
Plant	pine tree, cactus, tulip, tomato, ivy, maple tree	• many-celled • no structures for moving from place to place • make their own food • reproduce by seeds or spores
Fungus	yeast, slime mold, mushroom, mold	• many-celled; some one-celled • most don't have structures for moving from place to place • absorb food from other organisms
Protist	amoeba, paramecium, diatom, algae	• most one-celled; some many-celled • can make their own food or feed on other organisms • some have structures for moving from place to place
Moneran	bacteria	• very simple cells • some make their own food; some feed on other organisms • some have structures for moving from place to place

ANIMAL KINGDOM The clownfish and the orangutan look very different from one another. But they are both members of the animal kingdom. Like most kinds of animals, they move from place to place, often in search of food.

▼ orangutan

▲ clownfish

PLANT KINGDOM The largest members of the plant kingdom are trees. Trees, like other plants, use the Sun's energy to make food in their leaves. An oak tree can produce over a million leaves in a single year!

oak tree ▶

FUNGUS KINGDOM You might think these mushrooms look like plants, but they're not plants. They belong to a different kingdom— the fungus kingdom. Unlike plants, mushrooms can't make their own food. Most mushrooms get their food from the dead plant material on which they grow.

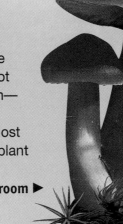

mushroom ▶

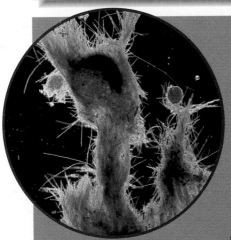

▲ paramecium

PROTIST KINGDOM A paramecium is a member of the protist kingdom. Like most other protists, the paramecium is made up of one cell and so is microscopic. Some protists have structures for moving from place to place. The paramecium has hairlike parts that pull it through the water.

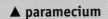

paramecium in pond water ▶

MONERAN KINGDOM Bacteria belong to the moneran (mə-nir'ən) kingdom. Unlike other monerans, blue-green bacteria make their own food. All monerans are made up of one cell.

bacteria cells that form a chain ▶

▲ blue-green bacteria

Internet Field Trip

Visit **www.eduplace.com** to learn more about how living things are classified.

Classifying— Past and Present

Reading Focus How has the way people classify living things changed since ancient times?

For over 3,000 years, scientists have looked for traits that would relate living things to one another. From about 350 B.C. to the mid-1900s, most scientists were content to classify organisms into just two groups—plants and animals.

But as science has advanced over the years, so have ideas about classifying organisms. The time line tells about a few of the people throughout history who have invented classification systems. Scientists continue to change classification systems as they learn more about living things.

Georges Cuvier classifies everything that can move from place to place on its own as a member of the animal kingdom.

1812

Aristotle, a scientist and teacher in ancient Greece, invents a system that places living things in two groups—plants and animals.

350 B.C.

1750s

Carolus Linnaeus, a Swedish scientist, develops a system for naming organisms that is still used today. He is known as the Father of Modern Classification.

Leon Roddy, an African American scientist, classifies more than 6,000 spiders and becomes a world expert on this group of animals.

1960s

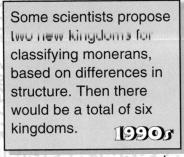

Some scientists propose two new kingdoms for classifying monerans, based on differences in structure. Then there would be a total of six kingdoms.

1990s

1988

Lynn Margulis, an American scientist, suggests a protoctist (prə tōk′tist) kingdom to replace the protist kingdom. This larger kingdom includes the protists as well as many-celled organisms that don't fit in the other four kingdoms. This system is not yet widely accepted.

1959

Robert Whittaker, an American professor of biology, introduces the five-kingdom classification system that is widely used today.

UNIT PROJECT LINK

For this Unit Project you will make a field guide to local plants or animals. With your group, choose the plants or animals to include. Find out information about each one. You might contact your state's Department of Natural Resources for help. Then put the information you gather in your field guide.

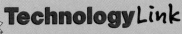 **Technology**Link

For more help with your Unit Project, go to **www.eduplace.com**.

Classification of Animals

Reading Focus Into what two groups are all animals classified, and how are the groups alike and different?

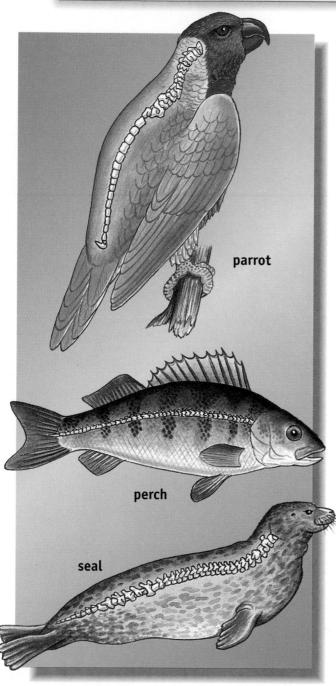

parrot

perch

seal

▲ Examples of vertebrates

Each organism in the animal kingdom moves on its own, is large enough to be seen without a microscope, gets its own food, and produces young. These few traits are common to all animals. The activity on pages C6 and C7 shows that different kinds of animals can have different traits. For this reason, scientists have further classified animals into smaller groups within the animal kingdom.

Who Has a Backbone?

Animals that have backbones make up one group. You can feel the knobs of your backbone down the center of your back. Each knob is part of a separate bone. Each bone that makes up the backbone is called a **vertebra**. Animals that have backbones are called **vertebrates** (vʉr′tə brits).

Vertebrates include many different kinds of animals. They can be found just about anywhere—in oceans, rivers, forests, mountains, and deserts. Horses, hippos, cats, birds, snakes, lizards, frogs, and fish are all vertebrates. All vertebrates have one thing in common—a backbone.

Life Without a Backbone

The members of many different animal groups don't have backbones. Animals that don't have backbones are called **invertebrates**. In fact, 97 percent of the animal kingdom is made up of invertebrates! They include some of the smallest animals, such as spiders, mites, and insects. Some invertebrates can be found in ponds, oceans, and other water environments where they can move about easily. Others have no trouble moving about on land or in the air.

Insects and some other invertebrates have exoskeletons (eks ō-skel'ə tənz). An **exoskeleton** is a hard outer covering that protects an animal's body and gives it support.

The animals within each of the major groups of the animal kingdom have many different traits. These major animal groups, then, are classified into even smaller groups. These groups are based on traits that the animals within the groups share. ■

Examples of invertebrates ▼

centipede

snail

INVESTIGATION 1 WRAP-UP

REVIEW

1. Name three kingdoms of living things. Name one organism that belongs to each kingdom.

2. Which group makes up most of the animal kingdom, vertebrates or invertebrates?

CRITICAL THINKING

3. An organism has no structures for moving from place to place. It makes its own food, and it reproduces by seeds. In what kingdom would you place this organism? Explain your answer.

4. As you pet a dog, you feel hard knobs along its back. What are these knobs? Based on this feature, into what group of animals would you classify the dog? Explain your answer.

HOW DO VERTEBRATES DIFFER?

A backbone, two eyes, and one mouth are some traits shared by a snake, a cat, and a human. But you probably can name many more ways in which snakes, cats, and people are different. In Investigation 2 you'll explore ways that vertebrates differ.

Activity

Cold Fish

How is the way a fish breathes different from the way you breathe? Find out what change might make a fish breathe faster or slower.

MATERIALS
- goldfish in large plastic jar
- thermometer
- timer
- ice cubes
- *Science Notebook*

SAFETY //////
Be careful when handling a glass thermometer.

Procedure

1. In your *Science Notebook*, **make a chart** like the one shown.

	Water Temperature	Breathing Rate
First reading		
Two minutes after ice cubes were added		

2. Your teacher will give your group a plastic jar with a goldfish in it. Use a thermometer to **measure** the temperature of the water. **Record** the temperature in your chart.

3. **Observe** two flaps behind the fish's eyes. Under the flaps are **gills**, which help the fish "breathe." The flaps open and close once with each breath. **Count** and **record** the number of breaths the fish takes in one minute. Repeat your counting several times. Then find the average of your results.

See **SCIENCE and MATH TOOLBOX** page H5 if you need to review **Finding an Average**.

Step 5

4. **Predict** how the number of times the flaps open and close in one minute will change if ice cubes are added to the water. **Record** your prediction. Gently place two or three ice cubes in the water in the jar.

5. Wait two minutes. Then **measure** the temperature of the water again. **Count** the number of times the flaps open and close in one minute. **Record** your observations. Repeat your counting several times and find the average. Remove the ice.

Analyze and Conclude

1. How does the temperature of the water affect how the fish breathes? **Compare** your results with your prediction.

2. Think about what happens when you go outside in very cold weather. Does your breathing rate change when you go from warm air into cold air? **Draw a conclusion** about how you are different from a fish, in terms of breathing.

Technology Link
CD-ROM

INVESTIGATE FURTHER!

Use the **Science Processor CD-ROM**, *Animals* (Investigation 2, Skin and Bones) to explore how the skeletons of fish, mammals, birds, reptiles, and amphibians are alike. Watch a video about how a backbone is useful. Learn about the body temperatures of different groups of animals.

Swim, Leap, and Slither

Reading Focus What traits are used to classify a vertebrate as a fish, an amphibian, or a reptile?

Has anyone ever told you that you're one in a million? Actually, as a vertebrate, you're one in several thousand. Vertebrates can be sorted into smaller groups, classified by traits that they have in common. Fish, amphibians (am fib′ē ənz), and reptiles are three of these groups.

Fish Tales

Did you know that fish are the largest group of vertebrates? There are more than 30,000 different kinds of fish in all. They come in many sizes and shapes, from the tiny minnow to the great white shark.

Many vertebrates that live in water are classified as **fish**. Most fish have body temperatures that vary with the temperature of the environment.

Most fish also have fins that help them steer and balance in the water. The feathery parts on the side of a fish's head are called **gills**. Water flows over the gills and allows the fish to "breathe" underwater. Many fish are covered with scales. Scales, which are hard, help protect fish.

Fish are vertebrates that live in water. ▶

Slippery Amphibians

There are almost 4,000 varieties of frogs, toads, salamanders, and other amphibians. An **amphibian** is a vertebrate that usually lives in water after hatching from an egg, but as an adult can live on land. The body temperature of an amphibian varies with the temperature of its surroundings. On land, amphibians live in wet environments. Some amphibians have smooth, moist skin, which makes them look and feel slippery.

Amphibians hatch from jelly-coated eggs. Their young usually do not look anything like the parents. Young amphibians start life with gills and breathe like fish. They even have tails that help them swim.

As they get older, amphibians grow legs and lose their gills. Adult amphibians breathe air with lungs. Frogs and toads lose their tails as adults, but salamanders keep theirs.

> **Using Math**
> *A wood frog develops from a tadpole in about 77 days. How many weeks is that?*

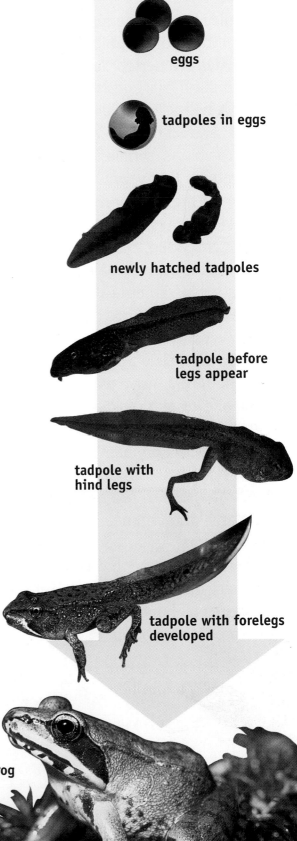

The Development of a Frog

eggs

tadpoles in eggs

newly hatched tadpoles

tadpole before legs appear

tadpole with hind legs

tadpole with forelegs developed

adult wood frog

Variety Is the Spice of Reptile Life

Reptiles have some features that differ from those of amphibians and fish. A **reptile** is a vertebrate that has dry, scaly skin and lays eggs that have a leathery shell. All reptiles lay their eggs on land, and all breathe air. Like fish and amphibians, reptiles have body temperatures that vary with the temperature of the environment.

Reptiles include animals as large as the Nile crocodile, 5.5 m (18 ft) long. They also include animals as small as the bog turtle, 10 cm (4 in.) long. Reptiles live in hot, dry deserts and in warm, wet tropical rain forests.

These animals vary in other ways as well. They may move as quickly as a rattlesnake or as slowly as a tortoise. Snakes are reptiles that slither. Some turtles swim underwater. Reptiles may or may not have tails or even legs. Lizards and snakes are able to shed their skins, and chameleons can change colors!

Fish, amphibians, and reptiles have some very different features. But these vertebrates all have one thing in common—a backbone! ■

▲ **Jackson's chameleon**

A crocodile is a reptile. ▼

Fly, Dive, and Gallop

Reading Focus What traits are used to classify a vertebrate as a bird or a mammal?

Besides fish, amphibians, and reptiles, there are two other groups of vertebrates with some very different traits. These are the birds and the mammals.

To Fly Like a Bird

There are about 9,000 types of birds in the world. **Birds** are vertebrates that have wings and are covered with feathers. These vertebrates lay hard-shelled eggs, which hatch in their nests. Birds range in size from the very small hummingbird, no bigger than your finger, to the large ostrich, taller than an adult human.

A bird's skeleton is very light in weight. Its bones are hollow. Having hollow bones helps to make the bird light enough to fly through the air. The fastest of all birds is the white-throated spinetail swift. This little bird can fly over 160 km/h (100 mph)!

No matter their size, their color, or where they live, all birds have feathers covering their bodies. No other group of animals has this feature.

A scarlet macaw ▼

◄ A bird's hollow bone

▲ A close-up view of a macaw's feathers

Using Math *A baby whale can drink 11 L (3 gal) of milk in less than five minutes. About how much milk is that in one minute?*

Our Group, the Mammals

Do you remember your first meal? It was milk, and it probably made you stop crying. Vertebrates that feed milk to their young and have hair or fur are called **mammals**. The young of most mammals grow inside the mother. When they have developed enough, the young are born live. But the young of the duckbill platypus, also a mammal, are not born live. Instead, they hatch from eggs.

You may not have realized that mammals include a wide range of animals. Apes, lions, hippos, dogs, elephants, kangaroos, squirrels, cats, pigs, bats, horses, rabbits, and even whales are all mammals. They're mammals because they all have hair or fur and feed milk to their young.

◀ **A squirrel is a mammal that can live in a city.**

C22

Most mammals have furry coats. Hair or fur traps a layer of air near the body, which helps the mammal stay warm. Humans don't have as much hair as other mammals. So wearing clothes helps people stay warm.

There are many different kinds of mammals in the world around you. The next time you watch a squirrel scramble up a tree or find a raccoon in your trash, remember that they're mammals, just as you are! ■

▲ The timber wolf pup will get a thicker coat of fur as it grows.

INVESTIGATION 2 WRAP-UP

REVIEW

1. What are the five groups of vertebrates? Name one animal that belongs to each group.

2. Give the traits of any two groups of vertebrates.

CRITICAL THINKING

3. Animal *A*, at a zoo where you work, comes from a rain forest. Animal *B* comes from a desert. Both lay eggs that do not have hard shells. Their body temperature varies with the temperature of the environment. To what vertebrate section of the zoo should you assign each animal?

4. Compare a salmon, a penguin, and a whale.

HOW DO THE GROUPS OF INVERTEBRATES DIFFER?

You learned that many animals don't have a backbone supporting their body. How are these animals without backbones grouped? Find out in this investigation.

Activity

Worming Their Way Home

Earthworms have no backbone and no eyes. How do you think these animals find their way around? How do they know when they are in their "home" environment? After doing this activity, you'll know how.

Procedure

1. Mark off four sections inside a cardboard box. Label the sections 1 through 4, as shown.

2. Place each material in a different section of the box, as shown in the diagram.

3. Remove the earthworm from its container and gently place it in section 1 of the box. With your group, **predict** which numbered section the worm will move toward. **Record** your prediction in your *Science Notebook*.

MATERIALS

- goggles
- cardboard box
- dry soil
- damp soil
- sand
- dry leaves or shredded newspaper
- hand lens
- earthworm
- timer
- *Science Notebook*

SAFETY

Wear goggles. Wash your hands when you have finished.

	Step 1
1 newspaper	2 dry soil
3 damp soil	4 sand

C24

Step 4

4. Using a hand lens, **observe** the location of the worm each minute for ten minutes. Also **observe** how it uses its body parts to move. **Record** your observations. When you finish observing the worm, gently place it back in its container.

 See **SCIENCE** and **MATH TOOLBOX** page H2 if you need to review *Using a Hand Lens*.

Analyze and Conclude

1. Into which sections did the worm move during the ten minutes? Which materials are in those sections? Where did the worm spend the most time? the least time?

2. **Describe** how the worm used its body parts to move.

3. **Compare** your results with your predictions. **Infer** the kind of environment earthworms like best.

INVESTIGATE FURTHER!

RESEARCH

Some people are using earthworms to recycle trash. Find out how worms are able to turn trash like paper into a useful material called compost.

Lifesaving Leeches

Reading Focus How were leeches once used, and how are they used today?

It may be brown, black, or covered with colored spots and stripes. It has 32 body segments and can grow as long as 45 cm (18 in.). What is it? It's an invertebrate called a leech. It feeds on the blood of other animals.

Doctors of the 1800s often used leeches to treat sick people. They believed that removing blood from a patient would help cure the patient's disease.

Today leeches have a different kind of role. Scientists have found that

chemicals in the saliva of a leech can prevent blood clots. Blood clots can cause a heart attack or a stroke. Scientists hope that the use of leeches will help prevent these life-threatening events.

Scientists have also found that damaged nerves in a leech can re-grow. By studying leeches, scientists may increase their understanding of nerves in humans.

In the past, people used leeches to cure almost any illness. ▼

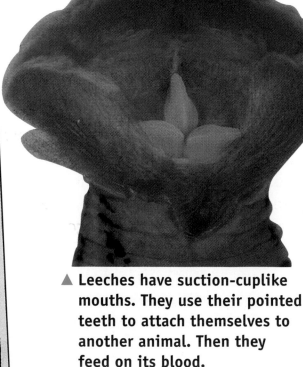

▲ **Leeches have suction-cuplike mouths. They use their pointed teeth to attach themselves to another animal. Then they feed on its blood.**

C26

Nothing Much in Common

Reading Focus What are the traits of some groups of invertebrates?

Some tumble along the ocean floor. Others glide through the water. Some burrow into the soil. Others fly through the air. The groups of animals without backbones are very different from one another. From spikes and soft bodies to claws and hard shells, you'll see how different some of these groups are.

Sponges

In the ocean you might mistake some animals for plants. Sponges are one group of invertebrates that look like plants. That's because they stay fixed in one place—on a rock, for example. Sponges are animals that have bodies full of holes and skeletons made of spiky fibers.

If a sponge can't move around, how does it catch a meal? Water flows through the holes of a sponge. Small pieces of food in the moving water become trapped in the sponge.

These animals, called sponges, ▶ look like plants. The holes in a sponge (*inset*) trap food for the animal.

Corals, Hydras, and Jellyfish

Corals may also look like plants, but they belong to another group of invertebrates. The animals in this group have soft, tubelike bodies with a single opening surrounded by armlike parts called tentacles. At night, corals feed by catching tiny animals in their tentacles.

Sea anemones (ə nem′ə nēz) and hydras also belong to this group. Sea anemones have tentacles that may look like the petals of a flower. But unlike flowers, sea anemones can move from place to place, gliding or tumbling along the ocean floor. Hydras are much smaller animals, with lengths of about 1 cm (0.4 in.). Like the larger animals in their group, hydras use their tentacles to trap food.

Jellyfish are part of the group that includes corals, sea anemones, and

▲ **Featherworm, a segmented worm that lives in the ocean**

hydras. If you've ever gone to the seashore, you may have seen jellyfish floating in the water or washed up on the sand. As a jellyfish drifts through the ocean, it catches shrimp, fish, and other animals in its tentacles.

Worms of Different Shapes

Worms are tube-shaped invertebrates. They can be found in both land and water environments. Worms are classified into groups by their body designs.

Although they may not look as if they belong, corals are members of the animal kingdom. ▼

Jellyfish shoot tiny poison darts from their tentacles to paralyze or kill their prey. ▼

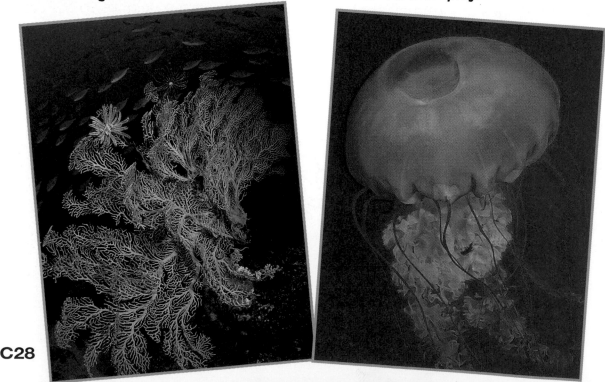

▲ Flatworm

▲ Roundworms

Flatworms are a group of worms that have heads and tails, and flattened bodies. A tapeworm is a flatworm that can live inside the body of other animals—even humans!

Roundworms are another group of worms. As you might guess, these worms have rounded bodies. They live in damp places and can also live inside humans and other animals. Both flatworms and roundworms can make people and other animals sick.

Another worm group, called the segmented worms, includes leeches and earthworms. The observation of the earthworm in the activity on pages C24 and C25 shows that an earthworm's body is divided into segments, or sections. All earthworms and other worms in this group have bodies made up of segments.

The earthworm activity also shows that the earthworm prefers burrowing through moist soil. In such a dark, damp environment, the earthworm can move easily and can keep from drying out.

Starfish and Sea Urchins

A starfish is an odd-looking underwater animal. It belongs to a group of invertebrates that have many tiny tube feet. Animals in this group have body parts arranged around a central area. The starfish shown has five arms and no head! It's hard spiny covering helps to give the animal protection.

The sea urchin belongs to the same group as the starfish. A sea urchin's body is covered with long spines. Like a starfish, it moves around on tiny tube feet.

Using Math
A starfish, such as the one shown here, can move over the sea floor at a rate of 10 cm (4 in.) per second. How far is that in one minute?

Shells Outside or Inside

The mollusks make up another group of invertebrates. A mollusk has a soft body, a hard shell, a rough tongue, and a muscular foot. A snail is a mollusk with a single hard shell protecting its soft body. A clam has two shells joined together by a hinge.

Squids and octopuses also belong to this group. But their hard shells are small and *inside* their bodies.

Lobsters to Butterflies

Arthropods are a group of invertebrates with jointed legs and hard exoskeletons that protect the animals. There are nearly 1 million known kinds of arthropods!

As an arthropod grows, it **molts**, or sheds its old exoskeleton. Then the animal grows a new, larger exoskeleton that allows its body to continue growing. A lobster is an arthropod with a thick exoskeleton.

Insects make up the largest subgroup in the arthropod group and include the only invertebrates that can fly. Insects, such as ladybugs, have bodies divided into three parts, and six legs arranged in three pairs. Most insects have two pairs of wings.

Like other arthropods, spiders have jointed legs. But spiders are *not* insects. Spiders have eight legs—two more legs than insects. They also have jaws and fangs!

◀ **An octopus is a mollusk.**

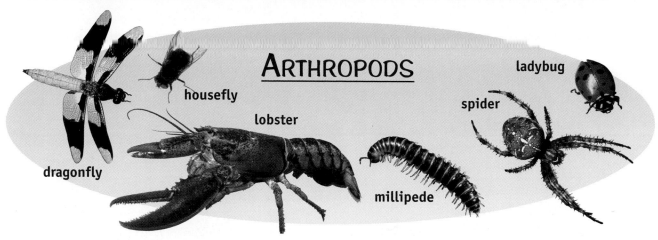

ARTHROPODS

dragonfly

housefly

lobster

millipede

spider

ladybug

Centipedes and millipedes are also arthropods. But they are not insects either. Centipedes can have up to 175 pairs of legs. They can use their many legs to run from enemies.

Millipedes can have up to 240 pairs of legs! But unlike centipedes, they don't use their legs to run from enemies. Instead, millipedes roll up their bodies when they sense danger approaching.

As you can now see, some of the groups of invertebrates are very different indeed. A sponge is very different from an arthropod. And a worm is very different from a jellyfish. But there is one way in which they are all alike—they have no backbone. ■

 **Arthropods can look very different from each other.**

UNIT PROJECT LINK

Make a drawing (or use a camera to take photos) of plants or animals for your field guide. Think about ways you can classify the plants or animals. How might you organize the descriptions and pictures in your guide?

TechnologyLink

For more help with your Unit Project, go to **www.eduplace.com**.

INVESTIGATION 3 WRAP-UP

REVIEW

1. What are eight of the groups of invertebrates? Name one animal that belongs to each group.

2. Give the traits of two groups of invertebrates.

CRITICAL THINKING

3. How could you use a mirror on this page to show that a spider has symmetry—that one half matches the other?

4. Normally, clotting stops bleeding. Suppose you have cut your finger badly. Might leeches play a role in helping stop the bleeding? Explain your answer.

HOW ARE PLANTS CLASSIFIED?

From an airplane high in the sky, a forest looks like just a sea of green. But up close, you can see that the forest is made up of many different plants. How are all these different plants classified?

Activity
Looking at Leaves

What traits can you use to classify plants? In this activity you'll classify plants according to their leaves.

Procedure

1. With your teacher's permission, go outdoors with a partner to **observe** the variety of plants.

2. Look at the trees, shrubs, flowering plants, and nonflowering plants. Choose five very different plants to examine closely. **Observe** the whole plant.

3. On a separate sheet of paper, draw each plant and one of its leaves. Place the drawings for each plant in a separate plastic bag. Label the bags 1–5.

4. Carefully remove a small sample of leaves from each plant. Place each sample in the bag with its drawings. Seal each bag. Take your samples back to class.

5. **Observe** the leaves on the plants you chose. Are the leaves needlelike or are they broad leaves that drop in autumn? Are their veins branched or do they run side by side down the length of the leaf? In your *Science Notebook*, make a chart like the one shown. **Record** your observations in the chart. Write each plant's name if you know it.

INVESTIGATE FURTHER!

RESEARCH

Use field guides to plants that are written for your region of the country. Try to identify the names of the plants you classified in the activity.

Classifying Leaves		
Bag	Leaf Characteristics	Group Name
1		

See **SCIENCE** and **MATH TOOLBOX** page H10 if you need to review **Making a Chart to Organize Data**.

Analyze and Conclude

1. Look at the information in the "Leaf Characteristics and Classification" table. Use the table to **classify** each plant you chose as one of the major plant groups. **Record** your classification in your chart.

2. **Compare** your conclusions with those of other groups. **Discuss** any differences in the way the plants were classified.

3. Which plant group is most common? Are there any plant groups you did not find examples of? If so, **infer** why.

Step 5

Plants to the Rescue

Reading Focus What are some ways that plants can be useful in the field of medicine?

SCIENCE TECHNOLOGY & SOCIETY Who usually answers a call for help? It might be a fire department or police department. It might be a paramedic or lifeguard. Would you ever expect it to be a plant?

You probably already know some ways that plants are used to help people. For example, plants are used to make clothing and shelter. And without plants, there would be no food. But did you know that plants are the source of most medicine?

Today, scientists search the world over for more plants used as medicine. The discovery of new medicines from plants is a costly business. But the business of healing is very important.

PLANTS USED FOR HEALING

GINKGO The leaves of the ginkgo tree are thought to help in treating Alzheimer's (älts′hī mərz) disease. This disease affects the way brain cells function. Ginkgo leaves are also believed to help relieve hearing loss, headaches, and asthma.

GINGER The root of this plant was used as long ago as the 16th century to settle upset stomachs. It has also been used for colds and flu.

PACIFIC YEW In the 1960s, scientists found a cancer-killing drug in the bark of the Pacific yew tree.

CHILIES Scientists have found that these peppers send signals to the brain to kill pain. Today a cream made from chilies is used to "rub out" pain.

GARLIC Garlic is used to help keep the heart and the blood vessels working properly. Except for medicines prescribed by doctors, garlic has become one of Europe's fastest-selling "medicines" for this purpose.

FOXGLOVE The medicine digitalis, from the foxglove plant, is used to stimulate the heart.

All Kinds of Plants

Reading Focus What traits are used to classify the members of the plant kingdom?

All plants are members of the plant kingdom. The family tree of the plant kingdom on this page shows that all plants are related. But in the activity on pages C32 and C33, different types of plants are shown to have different traits. Scientists use such differences to classify plants. For example, they divide the plant kingdom into two major groups: nonseed plants and seed plants. **Nonseed plants** do not reproduce with seeds. This group includes mosses and ferns. **Seed plants** do reproduce with seeds. This group includes plants that have flowers or cones.

Mosses and Liverworts

If you walk through a forest, you may notice a spongy carpet under-foot. This carpet is formed of mosses. **Mosses** are small nonseed plants that lack true roots, stems, and leaves.

Like other nonseed plants, mosses can reproduce by means of spores. Spores are one-celled structures that grow into new plants. Mosses also have male and female parts used in reproducing.

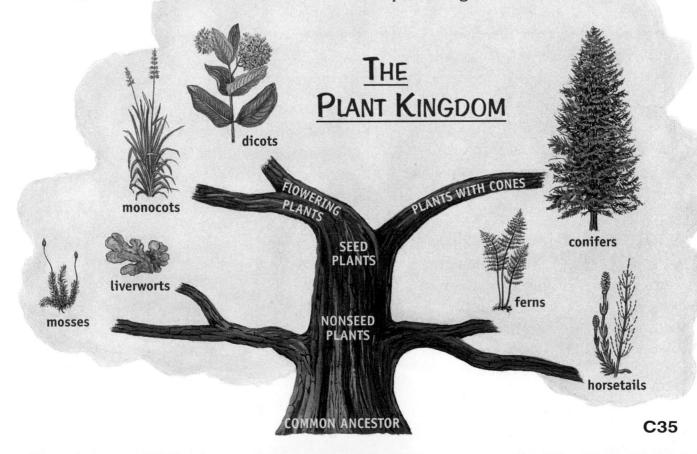

THE
PLANT KINGDOM

dicots

monocots

liverworts

mosses

FLOWERING PLANTS

SEED PLANTS

NONSEED PLANTS

PLANTS WITH CONES

conifers

ferns

horsetails

COMMON ANCESTOR

▲ Mosses produce spores at the tips of tall leafless stalks.

▲ The liverwort *Marchantia* produces spores on stalks with umbrella-shaped tops.

Mosses don't have special structures for carrying water. Because mosses lack such structures, water must move from cell to cell throughout the plant. This explains why mosses are small plants that are found growing only in moist places.

Liverworts are nonseed plants that lack true roots, stems, and leaves. Liverworts grow in moist places, such as along the banks of streams.

Ferns and Horsetails

Ferns are spore-forming plants that have roots, stems, and leaves. Before the dinosaurs lived, giant ferns covered much of Earth. Today, there are still many kinds of ferns. But they are not so common. They grow in very moist places that are not too hot or cold.

Like mosses, ferns reproduce by spores. They also have male and female parts used in reproducing.

Unlike mosses, ferns have special tubes that carry water from the roots to other parts of the plant. The roots of ferns anchor the plant in soil and carry water to scaly underground stems.

The most obvious parts of ferns are their leaves, called fronds. Some fern fronds appear to be made of many smaller leaves attached to a central stem. Actually, all of these smaller leaflike parts form one large fern frond. Spore cases are often produced on the undersides of the fronds. Spore cases contain spores.

Horsetails look more like paintbrushes than the tails of horses. About 30 species of horsetails live in marshes and swamps around the world. Like ferns, horsetails reproduce by spores and have underground stems.

Horsetails, nonseed plants ▶

Each spot on the underside of a fern frond is a cluster of spore cases. ▶

Living Math Suppose this ponderosa pine cone has 76 scales. Each pine cone can release 2 seeds per scale. About how many seeds could be released from this cone?

Conifers

Many plants, such as firs, produce seeds in cones. Cone-bearing plants are called **conifers** (kän'ə fərz). Like ferns, conifers have roots, stems, and leaves. However, conifers differ from ferns in the way they reproduce. Conifers reproduce by forming seeds. The seeds are located between the scales of protective cones.

Conifers may be small shrubs or tall trees. Huge forests of conifers cover much of the northern part of the world. Unlike other kinds of trees, most conifers keep their leaves in autumn. Many conifers, such as pines, spruces, and firs, have needlelike leaves. Others, such as cedar trees, have leaves that look like overlapping scales.

Science in Literature

LEAF TALK

EYEWITNESS • LIVING EARTH

Eyewitness Living Earth
by Miranda Smith
DK Publishing, 1996

"Leaves are so varied that botanists had to invent a whole new language to describe their shapes. . . . A plant living on the gloomy floor of a rain forest may need large leaves to catch enough sunlight. However, a plant growing on a mountaintop has plenty of light, but is battered by winds, and needs small, strong leaves to survive."

These words come from *Eyewitness Living Earth* by Miranda Smith. This book will amaze you with facts about all kinds of living things.

▲ The leaf of a hosta plant, a monocot, has parallel veins.

▲ The leaf of a cyclamen plant, a dicot, has netted veins.

Flowering Plants

Most of the plants familiar to you are flowering plants. Flowering plants are plants that have roots, stems, and leaves. These plants reproduce by seeds formed in flowers. As the seeds are formed, a fruit develops to cover and protect them.

A flowering plant may be classified as a monocot (män'ō kät) or as a dicot (dī' kät). A **monocot** is a flowering plant that produces seeds that are in one piece. The seed stores food for the developing plant. Corn plants are examples of monocots. Each kernel is a seed. A **dicot** is a flowering plant that produces seeds that have two sections. A lima bean plant is an example of a dicot.

One way to tell if a plant is a monocot or a dicot is to look at its leaves. The leaf of a mature monocot has veins that are parallel (par'ə lel). Parallel veins run side by side down the length of the leaf. The leaf of a mature dicot has netted veins. Netted veins form a branching pattern. You can see the two kinds of vein patterns in the pictures on this page.

Flowering plants are important. If you eat an orange or a carrot, you've eaten part of a flowering plant. On a summer day, you might cool off in the shade of a flowering plant, such as a maple tree. You might sit on a chair made of cherry wood. When you're sick, you might even take medicine made from flowering plants! ■

INVESTIGATION 4 WRAP-UP

REVIEW

1. What are the two main groups of plants?

2. Name the two main groups of seed plants. Give one example from each group.

CRITICAL THINKING

3. How are monocots and dicots alike and different?

4. In late autumn, you find a shrub that has no flowers. Its leaves are needlelike and green. How would you classify this plant? Explain your answer.

REFLECT & EVALUATE

Word Power

Write the letter of the term that best matches the definition. *Not all terms will be used.*

1. Vertebrates that have hair or fur and feed milk to their young
2. Seed plants that reproduce with cones
3. Feathery parts on the side of a fish's head
4. Each bone that makes up the backbone
5. Plants that have flowers or cones
6. Hard outer covering that protects an animal's body and gives it support

a. conifers
b. exoskeleton
c. gills
d. vertebra
e. mammals
f. mosses
g. seed plants
h. invertebrates

Check What You Know

Write the term in each pair that best completes each sentence.

1. Nonseed plants that look like paint-brushes are (dicots, horsetails).
2. Vertebrates are animals that have (backbones, exoskeletons).
3. An animal that lives in water after hatching but can live on land as an adult is (a mammal, an amphibian).
4. The leaves of dicots are (netted, parallel).

Problem Solving

1. Suppose you have discovered a new plant. How could the plant's leaves help you classify the plant as a fern, conifer, or flowering plant?
2. The body temperature of amphibians and reptiles varies with the temperature of their environment. How could this trait be a disadvantage for these animals?

BUILD YOUR PORTFOLIO

Look at the photograph to classify this organism. Write a paragraph or draw a diagram to explain your classification.

CHAPTER 2

THE SURVIVAL OF LIVING THINGS

How smart are the cats and dogs you know? They, like all other animals, have the ability to learn. They can learn behaviors that help them meet their needs for survival. All living things have those needs. And they have ways to meet those needs.

PEOPLE USING SCIENCE

Dog Trainer Ellen Torop at Canine Companions for Independence trains dogs to help disabled people. She can teach these "helping dogs" to follow about 60 commands. Thousands of disabled people depend on these well-trained animals. The helping dogs carry out simple, but important, tasks, such as turning lights on and off. They can push elevator buttons and carry items for disabled persons. Some dogs have even learned to push and pull wheelchairs.

Some of the animals are trained as "hearing dogs." They work with people who have hearing problems. Hearing dogs have learned how to alert their owners to important sounds, such as ringing telephones, smoke alarms, and doorbells.

In this chapter you'll find out more about all kinds of animals and about some of the things they learn to do.

◀ Dog trainer Ellen Torop's student learns to take a telephone to a disabled person.

WHAT ARE THE BASIC NEEDS OF LIVING THINGS?

Have you ever seen a duck put its head and neck underwater? The duck is looking for food. Food is one thing that all animals need. Find out in Investigation 1 about some other needs animals have in common.

Activity

Needs in Common

Scientists are trained to make careful observations. In this activity, see what you can find out about the needs of animals through careful observation.

- - - - - - - - - - - - - - - - -

Procedure

1. In your *Science Notebook*, **make a chart** like the one shown. **Identify** the animals pictured on pages C42 and C43. In your chart, **record** the names of the animals.

Animal	Need

See **SCIENCE** and **MATH TOOLBOX** page H10 if you need to review **Making a Chart to Organize Data**.

2. **Infer** what need each animal is trying to meet. Then **record** your inference in your chart.

Analyze and Conclude

1. How many different needs did you identify? Do some needs seem more important than others? Explain your answer.

2. Do all animals seem to share the same basic needs? **Predict** how the other basic needs of each animal shown might be met.

3. **Compare** your predictions with those of other group members. Explain each prediction you made.

The ABCs of Survival

Reading Focus What basic needs of living things can the environment provide?

If you had to take care of a pet dog, cat, and bird, how would you remember what each one needs? It wouldn't be very difficult. All three animals share a basic need for food and water.

Animals in the wild need food and water, too. What other basic needs do animals share? The activity found on pages C42 and C43 shows how some animals' needs are being met. Besides food and water, animals also need shelter to survive.

All animals need a suitable environment (en vī′rən mənt). An animal's **environment** is everything, both living and nonliving, that surrounds and affects the animal. To survive in its environment, an animal needs to keep

A hippopotamus spends much of its time in water. What does a hippopotamus eat? ▼

▲ The food of a killer whale includes penguins, walruses, and fish such as salmon, cod, and herring.

▲ A leopard takes its meal high up into a tree, where other animals cannot easily get at its food.

its body temperature within a certain range. This range varies, depending on the type of animal. In an environment that is suitable for an animal, that animal can meet all of its basic needs.

First, Some Food

All animals need food to grow, stay healthy, and survive. A mole dies after only a few hours without food! Other animals can wait an entire day for their next meal. Some animals, like snakes, can go for weeks without a meal.

Different animals eat different kinds of food. In the spring and summer, a rabbit feasts on plants such as dandelions and chickweed. But in the winter it settles for bark, roots, and dry leaves. A hippopotamus wanders out of the water to enjoy a meal of grass. A killer whale fills its stomach with fish, squid, sea birds, and even seals. Look at the photo caption to find out more about the foods a killer whale eats. A leopard hunts and kills other animals and then eats them while high up in the trees.

▼ A mole eats mainly worms and insects.

Some Water, Please

Plants and animals need more than just food to survive. They also need water. Many animals drink water every day from water holes, ponds, lakes, rivers, and streams. A budgerigar (buj'ər i gär), an Australian parakeet, can go a long time without taking a drink. But when it's time for that drink, the bird will probably flock together with tens of thousands of other budgerigars at one water hole.

A few animals hardly ever, or even never, drink! A kangaroo rat rarely drinks. It gets its water from the seeds and cactus pulp that it eats. An Australian koala never needs to drink. It gets the water it needs by eating eucalyptus (yo͞o kə lip'təs) leaves.

Using Math

This koala is eating leaves. A koala eats about 1 kg (2.2 lb) of leaves each day. Estimate how much it eats in one year.

▲ A flock of budgerigars visit a water hole to drink.

▲ Plants, such as these mangroves, need water to survive.

C46

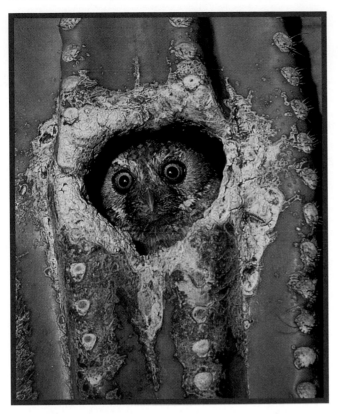

▲ **An elf owl finds a home in a cactus.**

example, many reptiles will lie in the sun if their body temperature is too cold. They will find shade if their body temperature is too hot. The body temperature of other animals stays within a certain range even while the temperature of the surroundings changes. Whether the air is hot or cold, your normal body temperature remains about 37°C (98.6°F).

As you can see, proper temperature, food, water, and shelter are some of the ABCs of survival for animals. Like animals, plants also need proper temperature, water, and shelter, or protection. But plants make their *own* food for growth. To do that, a plant needs energy from sunlight. For living things to survive and stay healthy, their needs must be met. ■

Home Sweet Home

Animals need shelter for protection from enemies and harsh weather. For example, the nest in which a baby bird hatches provides shelter for the bird. Young elf owls are kept safe in an old woodpecker hole in a cactus. A mouse can find shelter in a hole in the ground. Animals with hard coverings, such as turtles, carry their shelter with them.

Not Too Cold, Not Too Hot

An animal needs to live where its body temperature can be kept within a certain range. The body temperature of some animals changes with the temperature of the surroundings. For

UNIT PROJECT LINK

Think about each of the plants or animals you have decided to include in your field guide. What special parts do the plants or animals have to help them survive? What behaviors help them survive? Think of interesting ways to add these important facts to your field guide descriptions.

TechnologyLink
For more help with your Unit Project, go to **www.eduplace.com**.

weaverbird

The African Savanna

Reading Focus How does the environment of the animals of the savanna provide what they need to survive?

wildebeest

gazelle

wart hog

Wildebeests (wil'də bēsts) munch on grasses. Some drink from a water hole. Female lions hunting together catch a fast gazelle (gə zel'). A group of mongooses perch on a large termite mound made out of soil. These are some animals of the African savanna (sə van'ə). Like other animals, they need food, water, and shelter.

A **savanna** is a grassland found in tropical climates. It's a wide-open area that is covered with grasses but has only a few trees and bushes. Savannas cover almost one half of Africa. They are also found in India, South America, and Australia.

Food and Water in the Savanna

Like animals everywhere, animals of the African savanna need food. Zebras, wildebeests, and gazelles eat different parts of the grasses. The zebras feed on the tops of the grasses. Then wildebeests move into the area and feed on the middle parts. Later, gazelles chomp on the remaining bottom parts.

Giraffes eat the leaves of acacia (ə kā'shə) and baobab (bā'ō bab) trees. Secretary birds eat animals such as snakes and insects. Crocodiles in the water attack and eat wildebeests and other large animals as the animals try to cross rivers.

Animals of the savanna also need water. Many of them drink from the

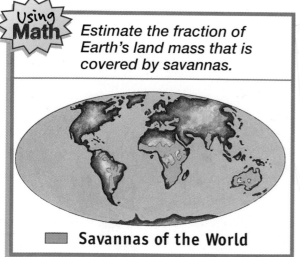

Using Math
Estimate the fraction of Earth's land mass that is covered by savannas.

Savannas of the World

acacia
tree

giraffe

zebra

rock hyrax

secretary bird

mongoose

same water hole. Some drink there once a day. Others only go there once in a while. Animals may also drink water from nearby rivers.

Savanna Shelters

Animals of the savanna need shelter, too. Rock hyraxes (hī′rak sez) live in holes in small hills of rocks called *kopjes* (käp′ēz). A wart hog's shelter is a large hole in an old termite mound.

Weaverbirds make nests of woven grasses that hang from tree branches. The opening to such nests is on the bottom. This design makes it more difficult for enemies to reach the birds inside.

Animals of all the world's savannas share the same basic needs. And although the animals all need the same things to survive, they must meet these needs in different ways. ■

INVESTIGATION 1 WRAP-UP

REVIEW

1. Baby birds have just hatched in a nest outside your window. Name three basic needs of the young birds.

2. How does a plant get the food it needs?

CRITICAL THINKING

3. How would a drought, or dry period, on the savanna affect a zebra's ability to meet its needs?

4. Think about the roles of animals of the savanna. Identify the animals that are meat eaters and those that are plant eaters.

INVESTIGATION 2

How Do Living Things Meet Their Needs?

What do teeth have in common with a bird's beak? Both kinds of body parts are used by animals to get food. In Investigation 2 you'll discover how the body parts and behaviors of living things help them meet their basic needs.

Activity

Feather Feats

A body covering is one of the body parts that help an animal meet its needs. A bird is covered with two types of feathers. Find out the purpose that each type serves!

MATERIALS
- tail or wing feathers
- down feathers
- hand lens
- *Science Notebook*

SAFETY
Wash your hands when you have finished this activity.

Procedure

1. Observe a tail feather or wing feather under a hand lens. In your *Science Notebook*, **make a drawing** of what you see.

 See **SCIENCE** and **MATH TOOLBOX** page H2 if you need to review *Using a Hand Lens*.

Tail feather ▼

barbs

central shaft

2. Work with group members to **identify** the central shaft and the barbs on your feather. Use the picture on page C50 for help. Gently pull some of the barbs apart. **Record** your observations.

3. Pull the feather through your fingers as shown. **Observe** and **record** what happens.

4. Repeat steps 1 and 3, but this time examine a down feather.

5. Wave the tail or wing feather through the air. Then do the same with the down feather. **Observe** how the two types of feathers push the air around them. **Record** your observations.

Analyze and Conclude

1. Compare the two types of feathers. In what ways are they alike? What differences did you observe?

2. Infer which type of feather would help a bird fly. **Infer** which type of feather would help a bird keep warm. Discuss your inferences with other members of your group. Explain your thinking.

▲ **Down feather**

INVESTIGATE FURTHER!

EXPERIMENT

Make a plan to find out about body coverings other than feathers. With your teacher's help, collect samples of different body coverings. Then use a microscope to examine them. Make a drawing of each type of body covering. List questions about what you observe under the microscope.

Activity

Tap, Tap, Tap

In this activity you'll test whether you can change the behavior of goldfish as they learn that food is on the way.

MATERIALS

- fish tank with water and goldfish
- fish food
- pencil
- *Science Notebook*

Procedure

1. In your *Science Notebook*, **make a chart** like the one shown. With your group, **observe** how goldfish move in their tank. In your chart, **record** the movement you observe.

Day	Conditions	Observations
1	Without tapping or food (step 1)	
	With tapping but no food (step 3)	
1–10	With tapping and with food (step 5)	Day 1 _____ Day 2 _____ Day 3 _____ Day 4 _____ Day 5 _____
10	With tapping but no food, at the end of two weeks (step 6)	

See **SCIENCE** and **MATH TOOLBOX** page H10 if you need to review **Making a Chart to Organize Data**.

Step 1

2. Talk with your group and **predict** how the behavior of the goldfish might change if you try to attract them by making a sound. **Record** your prediction.

3. **Test your prediction.** Use a pencil to tap gently ten times on one wall of the fish tank. **Record** what you observe. Look for any changes in the behavior of the fish.

4. Sprinkle some fish food on the surface of the water at one end of the fish tank. At the same time, have another student tap the wall of the fish tank near where the food is sprinkled. **Record** the behavior of the fish.

Step 4

5. Repeat step 4 each school day for two weeks. **Record** what you observe.

Math Hint *"Each school day for two weeks" means you will do this 10 times.*

6. At the end of two weeks, tap on the wall of the fish tank ten times, but do *not* put any food in the water. **Observe** and **record** the behavior of the goldfish.

Analyze and Conclude

1. With your group, **compare** what you observed during step 3 with what you observed in step 6. How did the behavior of the goldfish change?

2. **Hypothesize** about how a sense of hearing might help fish survive. **Compare** your hypothesis with hypotheses of other group members. Explain why you came up with the hypothesis you did.

UNIT PROJECT LINK

Create a plan to publish your field guide to local plants or animals. Think of different ways to present your facts, such as in a booklet, in a bulletin-board display, or on audiotape.

Technology Link

For more help with your Unit Project, go to **www.eduplace.com**.

The Survival Game

> **Reading Focus** How do body parts and behaviors help living things survive?

Have you ever wondered how penguins, birds that can't fly, use their wings? Animals have different parts, or adaptations (ad əp tā′shənz), that help them meet their needs. **Adaptations** are body parts or behaviors of living things that help them survive in a certain environment.

Wings, Trunks, and Teeth

What are some body parts that help an animal get food? A penguin's strong wings are terrific for paddling underwater. A penguin can chase after fish and squid at speeds up to 32 km/h (20 mph).

An alligator snapping turtle swims with its mouth open. At the end of its tongue is a pink flap that looks like a worm. When a fish swimming by tries to eat the "worm," the turtle eats the fish.

Animals also have parts that are adaptations for getting water. An elephant can use its tusks for drilling to underground water. Then it uses its trunk to lift the water to its mouth. Dogs use their long tongues to scoop up water into their mouths.

Animals get some water from their food. A vampire bat's food is the blood of another animal. The blood

▲ An alligator snapping turtle waits underwater for food.

▲ An elephant can use its tusks and trunk to get water.

▲ The ears of a fennec, a kind of fox, help keep the animal cool.

▲ An armadillo's covering is its shelter.

contains water. To get the blood, the bat sticks its sharp teeth into the skin of its prey.

Claws, Feathers, and Ears

Some animals have parts that serve as shelters or help them make shelters. Snails and armadillos have hard outer coverings. Pocket gophers have large front teeth, sharp claws, and flexible bodies. These adaptations help the gophers dig tunnels that shelter them.

Animals have parts that help provide a proper temperature for them. The fluffy down feathers used in the activity on pages C50 and C51 help keep a bird warm. The large ears of an animal such as an elephant or a fennec help keep it cool. Blood passing through the animal's ears gives off heat, cooling the entire animal.

Behaviors for Survival

Suppose you go to a park and see a dog and its owner playing with a ball.

When you walk over to pet the dog, the owner tells the dog to sit. The dog sits. Then the owner tells the dog to lie down. But just as the dog is beginning to lie down, a squirrel scampers past. The dog leaps up and runs after the squirrel. You have just observed some interesting **behaviors**, or ways living things act or respond to their environment.

Technology Link
CD-ROM

INVESTIGATE FURTHER!

Use the **Science Processor CD-ROM**, *Animals* (Investigation 1, Feed Me!) to discover how different animals use their body structures to get food. Watch a video about how mammals use their bodies to meet their needs.

▲ A mother crocodile cradles baby crocodiles in her mouth.

Animals sometimes respond in ways that are instinctive. **Instinctive behaviors** are behaviors that living things inherit from their parents. Other behaviors, called **learned behaviors**, develop after birth. When the dog in the park sits on command, it is performing a learned behavior. The owner taught the dog to sit when told. But the dog's owner didn't teach it to chase squirrels! Running after a squirrel is an instinctive behavior of dogs.

Internet Field Trip

Visit **www.eduplace.com** to learn more about animal behavior.

Chasing and Cradling

Both kinds of behavior—learned and instinctive—help animals survive. A young wolf is born with deer-chasing behavior but must learn how to catch the deer for food. As a pup, a wolf learns this behavior by chasing and jumping on other wolf pups and its parents. It also learns by watching other wolves catch deer.

Animals have behaviors that help them protect themselves or their young. When there is danger, a mother crocodile instinctively keeps her young safe by cradling them in her mouth and throat. When the danger is past, the crocodile spits out her young!

Unlike a crocodile, a newborn rattlesnake doesn't need help from a parent. It can defend itself. A young rattlesnake instinctively coils and strikes at danger, just as its parent does.

Spinning and Shivering

Different kinds of animals have different behaviors for getting food. Some spiders have the instinctive

◀ Wolf pups pounce on and playfully bite each other.

◀ **A spider spins a web that catches prey.**

move to cooler shady places. Birds and many other animals shiver when they're cold. This behavior warms up their bodies. ∎

behavior of spinning a silk web that catches prey. When an unlucky bee gets stuck in a spider's web, the spider bites the bee to paralyze it. The spider then wraps the bee in silk, preventing the bee from escaping.

Animals also have behaviors for keeping their temperatures within a certain range. Turtles and lizards bask in the sun to warm up. When their body temperatures get too high, they

Basking in the sun helps warm a lizard. ▶

Science in Literature

Snakes and Other Reptiles
by Mary Elting
Illustrated by Christopher Santoro
Simon & Schuster, 1987

BEWARE OF SNAKES!

"When an animal—perhaps a wild pig—comes to the stream for a drink, the snake moves suddenly. It grabs the pig's leg in its mouth. Then with swift looping motions it wraps itself in coils around the animal's body. The pig cannot move. Little by little the snake squeezes its coils tighter and tighter till the pig cannot breathe and in a short while is dead."

This description of an anaconda is from the book *Snakes and Other Reptiles* by Mary Elting. Read this book for more exciting tales of reptile survival.

Is It Ever Too Late?

Reading Focus What can happen if the needs of living things are not met?

A species, or group of living things that produce living things of the same kind, has many members. Some members may die out because their needs can't be met. Other members have characteristics that help them to survive. If the needs of *all* members of a species can't be met, that species becomes **extinct** (ek stiŋkt′), or dies out.

Organisms are produced, grow and mature, produce young, and then eventually die. But as long as an organism has produced young, its species will continue to exist.

To survive, an organism must be able to meet its needs in the environment where it lives. But environments differ. A polar bear cannot survive in a desert. It would die from the heat. But camels, who can live in desert heat with little water, can survive there. A camel cannot survive in the Arctic. It would die from the cold. But polar bears have a layer of fat that helps them survive the cold.

When Environments Change

Naturally caused forest fires, earthquakes, and long periods of drought or rainfall may change an environment. Then living things in that environment may die.

But not all living things die because of natural forces. Sometimes people change environments. Then the needs of plants and animals in that environment may no longer be met. When trees are cut down, many animals lose both their food and their shelter. Oil spills can ruin water environments. For example, crabs soaked with oil die. Then the animals that rely on the crabs as food also die.

▲ **Florida's 1998 forest fires destroyed the environment of many living things.**

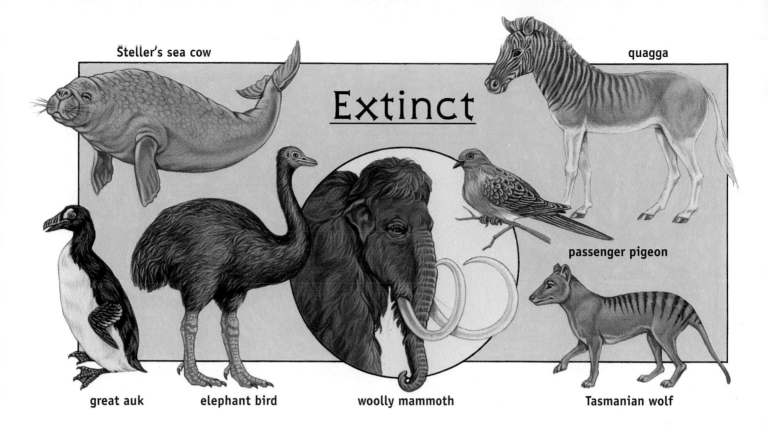

Steller's sea cow

Extinct

quagga

passenger pigeon

great auk   **elephant bird**   **woolly mammoth**   **Tasmanian wolf**

When It's Too Late

There are fewer than 50,000 Asian elephants left in the world. But because these animals do exist, it isn't too late for that species to survive. It is too late, however, for species that are already extinct. Some of these are shown on this page.

One species of extinct animal is the woolly mammoth. As you can see in the picture above, it looked very much like an elephant. Elephants exist today. But for 10,000 years, there have been no woolly mammoths.

Among extinct animals that lived before recorded history, dinosaurs are the most famous. Dinosaurs lived more than 50 million years ago. According to some scientists, today's birds are very similar to dinosaurs. Those scientists think that birds should be considered living dinosaurs. Dinosaurs were very

large reptiles. Even though there are no more dinosaurs, other reptiles, such as alligators and crocodiles, exist today.

When It's Not Too Late

Sometimes plants and animals become endangered, or scarce, because they are killed for use in products. Because snow leopards have been killed for their skins, these animals have become endangered. By law, endangered animals can no longer be hunted and killed.

On the island of Guam, brown snakes ate albatross young and their eggs until none were left on the island. On other islands in the Pacific, the albatross was hunted for its feathers. After a period of time, the species was declared extinct. Then a few remaining birds were discovered, so the albatross is not extinct after all.

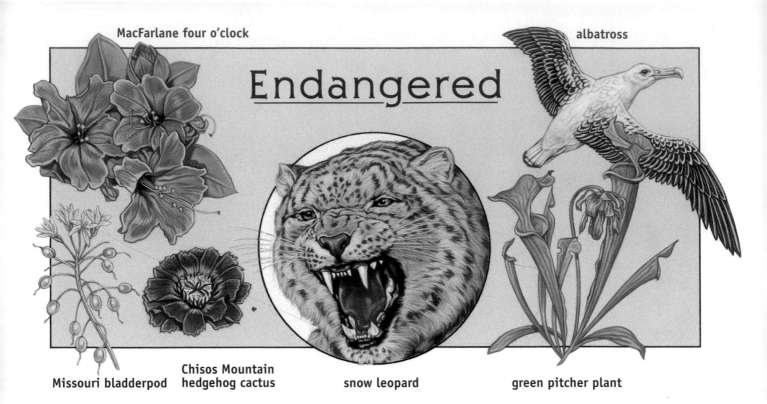

MacFarlane four o'clock

albatross

Endangered

Missouri bladderpod

Chisos Mountain hedgehog cactus

snow leopard

green pitcher plant

As long as some individuals of a species exist, it's not too late to save the species. People can help endangered species recover. It's not too late, then, for the snow leopard. It's also not too late for the fewer than 50,000 Asian elephants left in the world. For the albatross, it was almost too late.

A change in environment, whether natural or caused by people, affects living things. Living things in the environment can become endangered or even extinct. For extinct species, it's too late. But it's never too late for people to rebuild environments. And it's never too late for people to protect environments. ∎

INVESTIGATION 2 WRAP-UP

THINK IT WRITE IT

REVIEW

1. What is instinctive behavior? Describe an example of it.

2. Name two animals. Describe one behavior that helps each animal meet a basic need.

CRITICAL THINKING

3. Choose a circus animal. Describe one instinctive behavior and one learned behavior.

4. Think about the adaptations of animals that help them to survive. What traits might help some Asian elephants to survive?

REFLECT & EVALUATE

Word Power

Write the letter of the term that best completes each sentence. *Not all terms will be used.*

a. adaptations
b. environment
c. instinctive behaviors
d. learned behaviors
e. savanna
f. extinct

1. Behaviors that living things inherit are called ——.
2. Everything, both living and nonliving, that surrounds and affects an animal is its ——.
3. To die out is to become ——.
4. Behaviors that develop after birth are ——.
5. A grassland found in tropical climates is a ——.

Check What You Know

Write the term in each pair that best completes each sentence.

1. The basic needs of animals include food, water, proper temperature, and (learned behaviors, shelter).
2. An example of an extinct animal is the (elephant, dinosaur).
3. Body parts or behaviors that help living things survive in a certain environment are called (adaptations, instinctive behaviors).
4. Endangered animals are animals that have become (extinct, scarce).

Problem Solving

1. Suppose you take an imaginary trip to an African savanna. You see many different kinds of animals. Identify some of the things the animals of the savanna use for food.

2. On a cold day you see a bird sitting with its feathers fluffed out. It's shivering. What need is the bird meeting? What adaptations does the bird have to help meet that need?

BUILD YOUR PORTFOLIO

Study the photograph. Make a list of the armadillo's basic needs. Describe how the animal is meeting one of its basic needs.

Compare and Contrast

Making comparisons when you read helps you understand what a writer is saying. As you read, ask if two things or ideas are alike or different from each other.

Read the passages below. Then complete the exercises that follow.

> Look for these signal words to help you compare and contrast.
> - To show similar things: *like, the same as, in common*
> - To show different things: *different from, by contrast*

Who Has a Backbone?

Animals that have backbones make up one group. You can feel the knobs of your backbone down the center of your back. Each knob is part of a separate bone. Each bone that makes up the backbone is called a **vertebra**. Animals that have backbones are called **vertebrates**.

Vertebrates include many different kinds of animals. Horses, hippos, cats, birds, snakes, lizards, frogs, and fish are all vertebrates. All vertebrates have one thing in common—a backbone.

Life Without a Backbone

The members of many different animal groups don't have backbones. Animals that don't have backbones are called **invertebrates**. In fact, 97 percent of the animal kingdom is made up of invertebrates! They include some of the smallest animals, such as spiders, mites, and insects. Some invertebrates can be found in ponds, oceans, and other water environments where they can move about easily. Others have no trouble moving about on land or in the air.

1. What two things are being compared?

2. What is the main difference between the two things that are being compared? Write the letter of the answer.

   a. Where they live   **c.** How big they are

   b. How they move   **d.** Whether they have a backbone

Analyze Data

The average lengths in meters of various dolphins and whales are shown in this table.

Average Lengths of Dolphins and Whales

Type of Dolphin or Whale	Length (m)
Bottlenosed dolphin	3.9
Dusky dolphin	1.6
Humpback dolphin	2.4
Killer whale	8.0
Long-finned pilot whale	7.0
Melon-headed whale	2.6

Use the information in the table to complete the exercises that follow.

1. Which animal has the greatest length? the shortest length?

2. Which two types of animals, lined up nose to tail, would have a length of exactly 5 m?

3. Which animal is as long as five dusky dolphins lined up nose to tail?

4. About how many times longer is a killer whale than a bottlenosed dolphin?

5. The range of a set of data is found by subtracting the smallest number from the largest number in the set of data. What is the range of data in the table?

6. Estimate how many of your arm spans would equal the length of the killer whale.

WRAP-UP!

On your own, use scientific methods to investigate a question about living things.

THINK LIKE A SCIENTIST

Ask a Question

Pose a question about living things that you would like to investigate. For example, ask, "How can an animal's color help it survive?"

Make a Hypothesis

Suggest a hypothesis that is a possible answer to the question. One hypothesis is that an animal's color helps it blend into its environment so that predators cannot find it.

Plan and Do a Test

Plan a controlled experiment to find out if an animal's color helps it hide from predators. You could start with a large brown cloth, pipe cleaners in assorted colors (including brown), and a timer. Develop a procedure that uses these materials to test the hypothesis. With permission, carry out your experiment. Follow the safety guidelines on pages S14–S15.

Record and Analyze

Observe carefully and record your data accurately. Make repeated observations.

Draw Conclusions

Look for evidence to support the hypothesis or to show that it is false. Draw conclusions about the hypothesis. Repeat the experiment to verify the results.

WRITING IN SCIENCE
Summary

Write a summary of "The ABCs of Survival," pages C44-C47. Use these guidelines to write your summary.

- State the main ideas of the resource.
- Briefly list the main supporting details.
- Write a concluding statement that sums up the content.

SCIENCE and MATH TOOLBOX

Using a Hand Lens

A hand lens is a tool that magnifies objects, or makes objects appear larger. This makes it possible for you to see details of an object that would be hard to see without the hand lens.

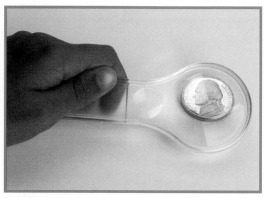

▲ Place the lens above the object.

▲ Move the lens slowly toward you.

Look at a Coin or a Stamp

1. Place an object such as a coin or a stamp on a table or other flat surface.

2. Hold the hand lens just above the object. As you look through the lens, slowly move the lens away from the object. Notice that the object appears to get larger.

3. Keep moving the lens until the object begins to look a little blurry. Then move the hand lens a little closer to the object until the object is once again in sharp focus.

If the object starts to look blurry, move the lens toward the object. ▶

Making a
Bar Graph

A bar graph helps you organize and compare data.

Make a Bar Graph of Animal Heights

Animals come in all different shapes and sizes. You can use the information in the table to make a bar graph of animal heights.

Heights of Animals	
Animal	Height (cm)
Bear	240
Elephant	315
Cow	150
Giraffe	570
Camel	210
Horse	165

1. Draw the side and the bottom of the graph. Label the side of the graph as shown. The numbers will show the height of the animals in centimeters.

3. Choose a title for your graph. Your title should describe the subject of the graph.

2. Label the bottom of the graph. Write the names of the animals at the bottom so that there is room to draw the bars.

4. Draw bars to show the height of each animal. Some heights are between two numbers.

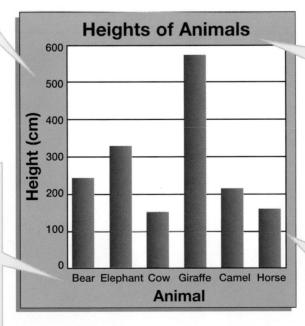

Using a Calculator

After you've made measurements, a calculator can help you analyze your data.

Add and Multiply Decimals

Suppose you're an astronaut. You may take 8 pounds of Moon rocks back to Earth. The table shows the weights of the rocks. Can you take them all? Use a calculator to find out.

Weight of Moon Rocks	
Moon Rock	Weight of Rock on Moon (lb)
Rock 1	1.7
Rock 2	1.8
Rock 3	2.6
Rock 4	1.5

1. To add, press:

(1) (.) (7) (+) (1) (.) (8) (+)

(2) (.) (6) (+) (1) (.) (5) (=)

Display: 7.6

2. If you make a mistake, press the clear entry key (CE/C) once. Enter the number again. Then continue adding. (Note: If you press CE/C twice, it will clear all.)

3. Your total is 7.6 pounds. You can take the four Moon rocks back to Earth.

4. How much do the Moon rocks weigh on Earth? Objects weigh six times as much on Earth as they do on the Moon. You can use a calculator to multiply.

Press: (7) (.) (6) (×) (6) (=)

Display: 45.6

5. The rocks weigh 45.6 pounds on Earth.

clear entry

divide

multiply

plus

equal

Finding an Average

An average is a way to describe a group of numbers. For example, after you have made a series of measurements, you can find the average. This can help you analyze your data.

Add and Divide to Find the Average

The table shows the amount of rain that fell each month for the first six months of the year. What was the average rainfall per month?

Rainfall	
Month	Rain (mm)
Jan.	102
Feb.	75
Mar.	46
Apr.	126
May	51
June	32

1. Add the numbers in the list.

$$
\left.\begin{array}{r} 102 \\ 75 \\ 46 \\ 126 \\ 51 \\ + \ 32 \end{array}\right\} \ 6 \text{ addends}
$$
$$
\overline{432}
$$

2. Divide the sum (432) by the number of addends (6).

$$
\begin{array}{r}
72 \\
6\overline{)432} \\
-42 \\
\hline
12 \\
-12 \\
\hline
0
\end{array}
$$

3. The average rainfall per month for the first six months was 72 mm of rain.

Using a
Tape Measure or Ruler

Tape measures and rulers are tools for measuring the length of objects and distances. Scientists most often use units such as meters, centimeters, and millimeters when making length measurements.

Use a Tape Measure

1. Measure the distance around a jar. Wrap the tape around the jar.

2. Find the line where the tape begins to wrap over itself.

3. Record the distance around the jar to the nearest centimeter.

Use a Metric Ruler

1. Measure the length of your shoe. Place the ruler or the meterstick on the floor. Line up the end of the ruler with the heel of your shoe.

2. Notice where the other end of your shoe lines up with the ruler.

3. Look at the scale on the ruler. Record the length of your shoe to the nearest centimeter and to the nearest millimeter.

Measuring Volume

A graduated cylinder, a measuring cup, and a beaker are used to measure volume. Volume is the amount of space something takes up. Most of the containers that scientists use to measure volume have a scale marked in milliliters (mL).

Measure the Volume of a Liquid

1. Measure the volume of juice. Pour some juice into a measuring container.

2. Move your head so that your eyes are level with the top of the juice. Read the scale line that is closest to the surface of the juice. If the surface of the juice is curved up on the sides, look at the lowest point of the curve.

3. Read the measurement on the scale. You can estimate the value between two lines on the scale.

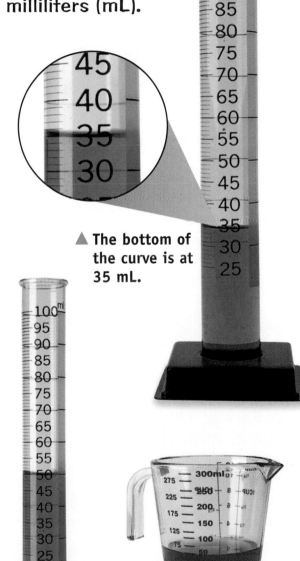

▲ The bottom of the curve is at 35 mL.

This beaker has marks for each 25 mL. ▶

This graduated cylinder has marks for every 1 mL. ▶

▲ **This measuring cup has marks for each 25 mL.**

Using a Thermometer

A thermometer is used to measure temperature. When the liquid in the tube of a thermometer gets warmer, it expands and moves farther up the tube. Different scales can be used to measure temperature, but scientists usually use the Celsius scale.

Measure the Temperature of a Cold Liquid

1. Take a chilled liquid out of the refrigerator. Half fill a cup with the liquid.

2. Hold the thermometer so that the bulb is in the center of the liquid. Be sure that there are no bright lights or direct sunlight shining on the bulb.

3. Wait a few minutes until you see the liquid in the tube of the thermometer stop moving. Read the scale line that is closest to the top of the liquid in the tube. The thermometer shown reads 21°C (about 70°F).

Using a
Balance

A balance is used to measure mass. Mass is the amount of matter in an object. To find the mass of an object, place it in the left pan of the balance. Place standard masses in the right pan.

Measure the Mass of a Ball

1. Check that the empty pans are balanced, or level with each other. When balanced, the pointer on the base should be at the middle mark. If it needs to be adjusted, move the slider on the back of the balance a little to the left or right.

2. Place a ball on the left pan. Then add standard masses, one at a time, to the right pan. When the pointer is at the middle mark again, each pan holds the same amount of matter and has the same mass.

3. Add the numbers marked on the masses in the pan. The total is the mass of the ball in grams.

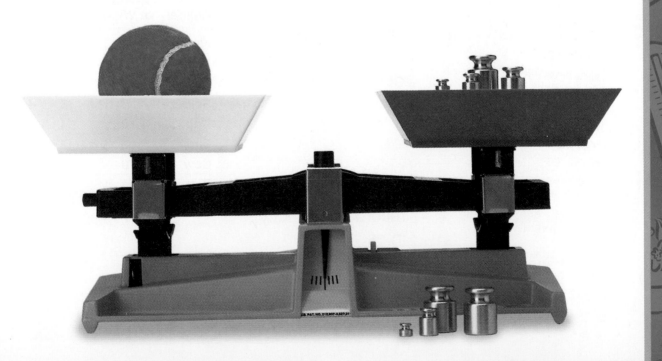

Making a Chart to Organize Data

A chart can help you keep track of information. When you organize information, or data, it is easier to read, compare, or classify it.

Classifying Animals

Suppose you are studying characteristics of different animals. You want to organize the data that you collect.

Look at the data below. To put this data in a chart, you could base the chart on the two characteristics listed— the number of wings and the number of legs.

My Data

Fleas have no wings. Fleas have six legs.

Snakes have no wings or legs.

A bee has four wings. It has six legs.

Spiders never have wings. They have eight legs.

A dog has no wings. It has four legs.

Birds have two wings and two legs.

A cow has no wings. It has four legs.

A butterfly has four wings. It has six legs.

Give the chart a title that describes the data in it.

Name categories, or groups, that describe the data you have collected.

Make sure the information is recorded correctly in each column.

Animals—Number of Wings and Legs

Animal	Number of Wings	Number of Legs
Flea	0	6
Snake	0	0
Bee	4	6
Spider	0	8
Dog	0	4
Bird	2	2
Cow	0	4
Butterfly	4	6

Next, you could make another chart to show animal classification based on number of legs only.

Reading a Circle Graph

A circle graph shows a whole divided into parts. You can use a circle graph to compare the parts to each other. You can also use it to compare the parts to the whole.

A Circle Graph of Fuel Use

This circle graph shows fuel use in the United States. The graph has 10 equal parts, or sections. Each section equals $\frac{1}{10}$ of the whole. One whole equals $\frac{10}{10}$.

Of all the fuel used in the United States, 4 out of 10 parts, or $\frac{4}{10}$, is oil.

Of all the fuel used in the United States, 3 out of 10 parts, or $\frac{3}{10}$, is natural gas.

Of all the fuel used in the United States, 2 out of 10 parts, or $\frac{2}{10}$, is coal.

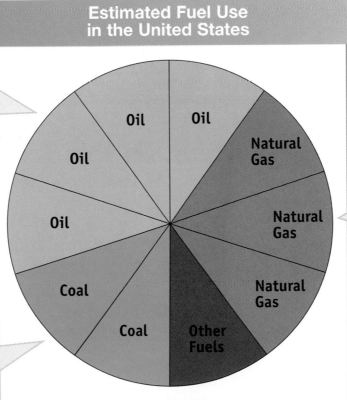

Estimated Fuel Use in the United States

Measuring Elapsed Time

A calendar can help you find out how much time has passed, or elapsed, in days or weeks. A clock can help you see how much time has elapsed in hours and minutes. A clock with a second hand or a stopwatch can help you find out how many seconds have elapsed.

Using a Calendar to Find Elapsed Days

This is a calendar for the month of October. October has 31 days. Suppose it is October 22 and you begin an experiment. You need to check the experiment two days from the start date and one week from the start date. That means you would check it on Wednesday, October 24, and again on Monday, October 29. October 29 is 7 days after October 22.

Monday, Tuesday, Wednesday, Thursday, and Friday are weekdays. Saturday and Sunday are weekends.

Last month ended on Sunday, September 30.

October

Sunday	Monday	Tuesday	Wednesday	Thursday	Friday	Saturday
	1	2	3	4	5	6
7	8	9	10	11	12	13
14	15	16	17	18	19	20
21	22	23	24	25	26	27
28	29	30	31			

Next month begins on Thursday, November 1.

Using a Clock or a Stopwatch to Find Elapsed Time

You need to time an experiment for 20 minutes.

It is 1:30 P.M.

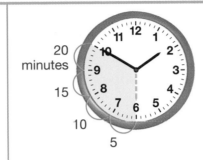

Stop at 1:50 P.M.

You need to time an experiment for 15 seconds. You can use the second hand of a clock or watch.

60 seconds = 1 minute

Start the experiment when the second hand is on number 6.

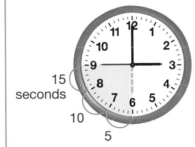

Stop when 15 seconds have passed and the second hand is on the 9.

You can use a stopwatch.

Press the reset button on a stopwatch so that you see 0:00 00.

Press the start button. When you see 0:15 00, press the stop button.

MEASUREMENTS

Volume
1 L of sports drink is a little more than 1 qt.

Area
A basketball court covers about 4,700 ft². It covers about 435 m².

Mass and Weight
A basketball has a mass of about 650 g. It weighs about $1\frac{1}{2}$ lb.

Metric Measures

Temperature
Ice melts at 0 degrees Celsius (°C)

Water freezes at 0°C

Water boils at 100°C

Length and Distance
1,000 meters (m) = 1 kilometer (km)

100 centimeters (cm) = 1 m

10 millimeters (mm) = 1 cm

Force
1 newton (N) =
  1 kilogram x meter/second/second
  (kg x m/s²)

Volume
1 cubic meter (m³) = 1 m x 1 m x 1 m

1 cubic centimeter (cm³) =
  1 cm x 1 cm x 1 cm

1 liter (L) = 1,000 milliliters (mL)

1 cm³ = 1 mL

Area
1 square kilometer (km²) = 1 km x 1 km

1 hectare = 10,000 m²

Mass
1,000 grams (g) = 1 kilogram (kg)

1,000 milligrams (mg) = 1 g

Temperature
The temperature at an indoor basketball game might be 25°C, which is 77°F.

Length/Distance
A basketball rim is about 10 ft high, or a little more than 3 m from the floor.

Customary Measures

Temperature
Ice melts at 32 degrees Fahrenheit (°F)
Water freezes at 32°F
Water boils at 212°F

Length and Distance
12 inches (in.) = 1 foot (ft)
3 ft = 1 yard (yd)
5,280 ft = 1 mile (mi)

Weight
16 ounces (oz) = 1 pound (lb)
2,000 pounds = 1 ton (T)

Volume of Fluids
8 fluid ounces (fl oz) = 1 cup (c)
2 c = 1 pint (pt)
2 pt = 1 quart (qt)
4 qt = 1 gallon (gal)

Metric and Customary Rates
km/h = kilometers per hour
m/s = meters per second
mph = miles per hour

GLOSSARY

Pronunciation Key

Symbol	Key Words
a	cat
ā	ape
ä	cot, car
e	ten, berry
ē	me
i	fit, here
ī	ice, fire
ō	go
ô	fall, for
oi	oil
o͞o	look, pull
o͞o	tool, rule
ou	out, crowd
u	up
ʉ	fur, shirt
ə	a in ago
	e in agent
	i in pencil
	o in atom
	u in circus
b	bed
d	dog
f	fall

Symbol	Key Words
g	get
h	help
j	jump
k	kiss, call
l	leg
m	meat
n	nose
p	put
r	red
s	see
t	top
v	vat
w	wish
y	yard
z	zebra
ch	chin, arch
ŋ	ring, drink
sh	she, push
th	thin, truth
th	then, father
zh	measure

A heavy stress mark (′) is placed after a syllable that gets a heavy, or primary, stress, as in **picture** (pik′chər).

adaptation (ad əp tā'shən) A part or behavior that makes a living thing better able to survive in its environment. (C54) The spider's behavior of spinning a web to catch an insect, such as a bee, is an *adaptation* that helps the spider get food

air (er) The invisible, odorless, and tasteless mixture of gases that surrounds Earth. (E10) *Air* consists mainly of the gases nitrogen and oxygen.

air mass (er mas) A large body of air that has about the same temperature, air pressure, and moisture throughout. (E62) When warm and cold *air masses* meet, the weather changes.

air pressure (er presh'ər) The push of the air in all directions against its surroundings. (E31) You can see the effect of *air pressure* when you blow up a balloon.

amphibian (am fib'ē ən) A vertebrate that usually lives in water in the early part of its life; it breathes with gills and then later develops lungs. (C19) Frogs, toads, and salamanders are *amphibians*.

anemometer (an ə mäm'ət ər) A device used to measure the speed of the wind. (E39) The *anemometer* showed that the wind was blowing at 33 km/h.

atmosphere (at'məs fir) The blanket of air that surrounds Earth, reaching to about 700 km above the surface. (E12) Earth's *atmosphere* makes it possible for life to exist on the planet.

atom (at'əm) The smallest part of an element that still has the properties of that element. (B30) Water forms when *atoms* of the elements hydrogen and oxygen combine in a certain way.

axis (ak'sis) An imaginary straight line from the North Pole, through Earth's center, to the South Pole. (E78) Earth makes one complete turn on its *axis* in about 24 hours.

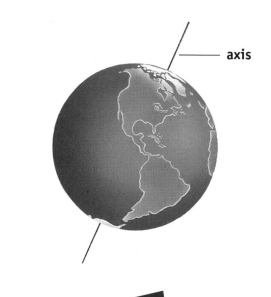

axis

barometer (bə räm'ət ər) A device used to measure air pressure. (E30) Scientists use a *barometer* to gather information about the weather.

bay (bā) Part of a sea or lake extending into the land. (A14) The ship sailed through the *bay* into the Atlantic Ocean.

behavior (bē hāv'yər) The way in which a living thing acts or responds to its environment. (C55) Purring, washing themselves, and hunting mice are three common *behaviors* of cats.

bird (bʉrd) A vertebrate that has wings, is covered with feathers, and hatches from a hard-shell egg. (C21) A *bird* is the only organism in the animal kingdom that has feathers covering its body.

boiling (boil'iŋ) The rapid change of state from a liquid to a gas. (B40) When water is *boiling*, bubbles of water vapor form.

carbon dioxide (kär'bən dī- äks'īd) A colorless, odorless gas. (E10) Plants use *carbon dioxide* from the air in the process of making food.

chemical change (kem'i kəl chānj) A change in matter that results in one or more different kinds of matter forming. (B56) A *chemical change* occurs when matter, such as paper, burns and forms gases and ash.

chemical formula (kem'i kəl fôr'myoo lə) A group of symbols that shows the kinds and number of atoms in a single unit of a compound. (B35) The *chemical formula* for carbon dioxide is CO_2.

chemical property (kem'i kəl präp'ər tē) A characteristic of a substance that can only be seen when the substance changes and a new substance is formed; describes how matter reacts with other matter. (B13, B56) A *chemical property* of iron is that iron can combine with oxygen to form rust.

chemical reaction (kem'i kəl rē ak'shən) The process in which one or more substances are changed into one or more different substances. (B57) A *chemical reaction* takes place when burning wood changes to ash.

chemical symbol (kem'i kəl sim'bəl) One or two letters that stand for the name of an element. (B30) The *chemical symbol* for gold is *Au*.

circuit breaker (sur'kit brāk'ər) A switch that opens or closes a circuit by turning off or on. (D52) When a circuit overheats, the *circuit breaker* switches off and the lights go out.

cirrus cloud (sir'əs kloud) A thin, feathery cloud made up of ice crystals high in the sky. (E57) *Cirrus clouds* often look like wisps of hair.

climate (klī'mət) The average weather conditions of an area over a long period of time. (E84) Some regions have a hot, rainy *climate*.

cloud (kloud) A mass of tiny droplets of water that condensed from the air. (E46) A dark *cloud* blocked the sunlight.

cold front (kōld frunt) The leading edge of a cold air mass that forms as the cold air mass moves into a warm air mass. (E62) Thunderstorms often occur along a *cold front*.

compass (kum'pəs) A device containing a magnetized needle that moves freely and is used to show direction. (D23) The north pole of the needle in a *compass* points toward Earth's magnetic north pole.

compound (käm′pound)
Matter made up of two or more elements chemically combined. (B33) Salt is a *compound* made up of sodium and chlorine.

condensation (kän dən sā′shən)
The change of state from a gas to a liquid. (B42) Drops of water form on the outside of a very cold glass because of the *condensation* of water vapor in the air.

condense (kən dens′) To change from a gas to a liquid. (E46) Water vapor from the air *condenses* on a cold window.

conductor (kən duk′tər) A material through which electricity moves easily. (D42) Copper wire is a good *conductor* of electricity.

conifers (kän′ə fərz) Cone-bearing plants. (C37) Pines and fir trees are examples of *conifers*.

conservation (kän sər vā′shən)
The preserving and wise use of natural resources. (A31) The *conservation* of forests is important to both humans and wildlife.

controlled experiment (kən-trōld′ ek sper′ə mənt) A test of a hypothesis in which the setups are identical in all ways except one. (S7) In the *controlled experiment*, one beaker of water contained salt.

cumulus cloud (kyo͞o′myo͞o ləs kloud) A large puffy cloud. (E55) White *cumulus clouds* can often be seen in an otherwise clear summer sky.

delta (del′tə) A flat, usually triangular plain formed by deposits of sediment where a river empties into the ocean. (A12) The largest *delta* in the United States is at the mouth of the Mississippi River.

density (den′sə tē) The property that describes how much matter is in a given space, or volume. (B9, B11) The *density* of air varies with its temperature.

dicot (dī′kät) A flowering plant that produces seeds that have two sections. (C38) A trait of a *dicot* is that the veins of its leaves form a branching pattern.

electric cell (ē lek′trik sel) A device that changes chemical energy to electrical energy. (D60) A battery in a flashlight consists of one or more *electric cells*.

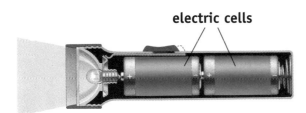

electric cells

electric charge (ē lek′trik chärj) The electrical property of particles of matter; an electric charge can be positive or negative. (D30) Rubbing a balloon with a wool cloth causes negative *electric charges* to move from the wool to the balloon.

electric circuit (ē lek′trik sur′kit) A path along which an electric current can move. (D41) We made an *electric circuit,* using a battery, wires, and a light bulb.

electric current (ē lek′trik kur′ənt) A continuous flow of electric charges. (D41) *Electric current* in wires allows you to run electric appliances, such as an iron or refrigerator, in your home.

electric discharge (ē lek′trik dis′chärj) The loss or release of an electric charge. (D33) A bolt of lightning is an *electric discharge*.

electromagnet (ē lek′trō mag nit) A magnet made when an electric current passes through a wire coiled around an iron core. (D70) A large *electromagnet* can be strong enough to lift heavy metal objects such as cars.

element (el′ə mənt) Matter made up of only one kind of atom. (B30) Iron, oxygen, and aluminum are three examples of *elements*.

energy (en′ər jē) The ability to cause change. (B39) Most automobiles use *energy* from gasoline to move.

environment (en vī′rən mənt) Everything that surrounds and affects a living thing. (C44) Desert animals and forest animals live in very different *environments*.

equator (ē kwāt′ər) An imaginary line circling the middle of Earth, halfway between the North Pole and the South Pole. (E78) The *equator* divides Earth into the Northern Hemisphere and the Southern Hemisphere.

erosion (ē rō′zhən) The gradual wearing away and removing of rock material by forces such as moving water, wind, and moving ice. (A10) Ocean waves cause *erosion* of the seashore.

evaporate (ē vap′ə rāt) To change from a liquid to a gas. (E46) Some of the water boiling in the pot *evaporated*.

evaporation (ē vap ə rā′shən) The change of state from a liquid to a gas. (B40) Under the hot sun, water in a puddle changes to water vapor through the process of *evaporation*.

exoskeleton (eks ō skel′ə tən) A hard outer structure, such as a shell, that protects or supports an animal's body. (C15) A lobster has a thick *exoskeleton*.

extinct (ek stiŋkt′) No longer living as a species. (C58) Traces of some *extinct* species can be found in fossils.

ferns (fɵrnz) Spore-forming plants that have roots, stems, and leaves. (C36) *Ferns* that grow in tropical places have very tall fronds.

filament (fil′ə mənt) A long, thin coil of wire that glows when electricity passes through it. (D48) The *filament* in an incandescent light bulb gives off light.

filament

fish (fish) A vertebrate that lives in water and has gills used for breathing and fins used for swimming. (C18) Sharks and tuna are kinds of *fish*.

flash flood (flash flɵd) A sudden, violent flood. (E67) Heavy rains caused *flash floods* as the stream overflowed.

fog (fôg) A cloud that touches Earth's surface. (E46) Traffic accidents often increase where *fog* is heavy.

fossil fuel (fäs′əl fyōō′əl) A fuel that formed from the remains of once-living things and that is nonrenewable. (A47) Oil is a *fossil fuel*.

freezing (frēz′iŋ) The change of state from a liquid to a solid. (B42) Water turns to ice by *freezing*.

front (frunt) The place where two air masses meet. (E62) Forecasters watch the movement of *fronts* to help predict the weather.

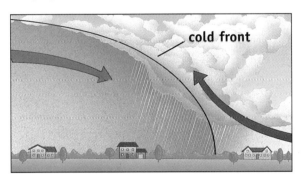

cold front

fuse (fyōōz) A device in a circuit that contains a metal strip, which melts when the circuit is overheated, thus breaking the circuit. (D52) The *fuse* blew because too many appliances were connected to the same electric circuit.

gas (gas) The state of matter that has no definite shape or volume. (B29) Helium is a very light *gas* that is used to fill some balloons.

generator (jen′ər āt ər) A device that changes energy of motion into electrical energy. (D58) The huge *generator* uses water power to produce electricity.

gill (gil) A feathery structure on each side of a fish's head that lets the fish breathe underwater. (C18) A fish takes in oxygen through its *gills*.

glacier (glā′shər) A huge mass of slow-moving ice that forms over land; glaciers form in areas where the amount of snow that falls is more than the amount of snow that melts. (A22) As it moves, a *glacier* changes the surface beneath it.

greenhouse effect (grēn′hous e fekt′) The process by which heat from the Sun builds up near Earth's surface and is trapped by the atmosphere. (E15) Some scientists fear that air pollution may increase the *greenhouse effect* and raise temperatures on Earth.

hazardous waste (haz′ər dəs wāst) A waste material that dirties the environment and that can kill living things or cause disease. (A65) Some chemicals used to kill insects become *hazardous wastes*.

headland (hed′land) A piece of land that extends out into the water and usually slows down the flow of water that passes it. (A14) The lighthouse stood on a *headland* overlooking the bay.

high-pressure area (hī presh′ər er′ē ə) An area of higher air pressure than that of the surrounding air. (E33) Winds move from *high-pressure areas* to low-pressure areas.

horsetails (hôrs tālz) Plants that reproduce by spores and have underground stems. (C36) *Horsetails* are also known as scouring rushes because of the tough tip at the end of their bamboo-like stem.

humidity (hyo͞o mid′ə tē) The amount of water vapor in the air. (E47) Tropical climates have warm temperatures and high *humidity*.

hurricane (hʉr′i kān) A large, violent storm accompanied by strong winds and, usually, heavy rain. (E70) The winds of the *hurricane* blew at over 125 km/h.

hypothesis (hī päth′ə sis) An idea about or explanation of how or why something happens. (S6) The *hypothesis* about the expanding universe has been supported by evidence gathered by astronomers.

ice age (īs āj) A period of time when glaciers covered much of Earth's land. (E89) During the last *ice age*, glaciers covered parts of North America.

incineration (in sin ər ā′shən) Burning to ashes. (A60) You can get rid of trash by *incineration*.

instinctive behavior (in stiŋk′tiv bē hāv′yər) A behavior that a living thing does naturally without having to learn it. (C56) For a mother bird, feeding her young is an *instinctive behavior*.

insulator (in′sə lāt ər) A material through which electricity does not move easily. (D42) Rubber can prevent an electric shock because rubber is a good *insulator*.

invertebrate (in vʉr′tə brit) An animal that does not have a backbone. (C15) *Invertebrates* include jellyfish, sponges, insects, and worms.

landfill (land'fil) An area where trash is buried and covered over with dirt. (A59) In some places, towns decide to build recreation areas, such as parks, on the sites of old *landfills*.

learned behavior (lʉrnd bē-hāv'yər) A behavior that an organism is taught or learns from experience. (C56) Sitting on command, catching a ball, and jumping through a hoop are examples of *learned behavior* for a dog.

lines of force (līnz uv fôrs) The lines that form a pattern showing the size and shape of a magnetic force field. (D19) Iron filings sprinkled over a magnet form *lines of force* that show the strength and the direction of the magnet's force.

liquid (lik'wid) The state of matter that has a definite volume but no definite shape. (B29) A *liquid*, such as water or milk, takes the shape of its container.

litter (lit'ər) The trash that is discarded on the ground or in water rather than being disposed of properly. (A66) The children cleaned up the park by removing all the *litter* they could find.

liverworts (liv'ər wʉrts) Nonseed plants that lack true roots, stems, and leaves. (C36) The logs by the stream were covered with mosslike *liverworts*.

lodestone (lōd'stōn) A naturally magnetic mineral found at or near Earth's surface. (D22) A piece of *lodestone* will attract iron.

low-pressure area (lō presh'ər er'ē ə) An area of lower air pressure than that of the surrounding air. (E33) Storms are more likely to occur in *low-pressure areas*.

magnet (mag'nit) An object that has the property of attracting certain materials, mainly iron and steel. (D11) The girl used a horseshoe *magnet* to pick up paper clips.

magnetic field (mag net'ik fēld) The space around a magnet within which the force of the magnet can act. (D20) The magnet attracted all the pins within its *magnetic field*.

magnetism (mag′nə tiz əm) A magnet's property of attracting certain materials, mainly iron and steel. (D11) *Magnetism* keeps kitchen magnets attached to a refrigerator door.

mammal (mam′əl) A vertebrate, such as a cat, that has hair or fur and feeds its young with milk. (C22) Dogs, cats, rabbits, deer, bats, horses, mice, elephants, whales, and humans are all *mammals*.

mass (mas) The amount of matter that something contains. (B10) A large rock has more *mass* than a small rock that is made of the same material.

matter (mat′ər) Anything that has mass and takes up space. (B10) Rocks, water, and air are three kinds of *matter*.

melting (melt′iŋ) The change of state from a solid to a liquid. (B40) As the temperature of the air rises, snow and ice change to liquid water by the process of *melting*.

metric system (me′trik sis′təm) A system of measurement in which the number of smaller parts in each unit is based on the number 10 and multiples of 10. (B20) Centimeters, meters, and kilometers are units of length in the *metric system*.

mineral (min′ər əl) A solid, found in nature, that has a definite chemical makeup. (A41) Salt, coal, diamond, and gold are some examples of *minerals*.

mixture (miks′chər) Matter that is made up of two or more substances that can be separated by physical means. (B50) This salad contains a *mixture* of lettuce, cucumbers, celery, and tomatoes.

molt (mōlt) To shed an outer covering such as hair, outer skin, horns, or feathers at certain times. (C30) Snakes and insects *molt*.

monocot (män′ō kät) A flowering plant that produces seeds that are in one piece. (C38) About one third of all flowering plants are *monocots*.

mosses (môs′əs) Small nonseed plants that lack true roots, stems, and leaves. (C35) The leaflike part of *mosses* grows only a few centimeters above ground.

natural resource (nach'ər əl rē'sôrs) Any useful material from Earth, such as water, oil, and minerals. (A31) One reason that trees are an important *natural resource* is that their wood is used to build houses and to make paper.

nitrogen (nī'trə jən) A colorless, odorless, tasteless gas that makes up about four fifths of the air. (E10) *Nitrogen* is used by plants for growth.

nonrenewable resource (nän-ri nōō'ə bəl rē'sôrs) A natural resource that can't be replaced once it's removed. (A42) Minerals are classified as a *nonrenewable resource* because there's a limited amount of them.

nonseed plants (nän sēd plants) Plants that do not reproduce with seeds. (C35) Ferns are *nonseed plants*.

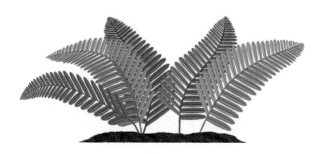

Northern Hemisphere (nôr'thərn hem'i sfir) The half of Earth north of the equator. (E79) Canada is in the *Northern Hemisphere*.

north pole (nôrth pōl) One of the ends of a magnet where the magnetic force is strongest; it points to the north when the magnet moves freely. (D13) *North poles* of magnets repel each other.

north pole

ore (ôr) A mineral or rock that contains enough of a metal to make mining that metal profitable. (A41) Gold, aluminum, copper, and tin come from *ores*.

organism (ôr'gə niz əm) A living thing that can be classified as belonging to one of several kingdoms. (C8) Animals and plants are *organisms*.

oxygen (äks'i jən) A colorless, odorless, tasteless gas that makes up about one fifth of the air. (E10) *Oxygen* is essential to life.

packaging (pak′ij iŋ) The wrapping and containers in which items are transported or offered for sale. (A75) *Packaging* protects products from damage but adds to their cost.

parallel circuit (par′ə lel sʉr′kit) An electric circuit having more than one path along which electric current can travel. (D51) Because the circuits in a home are *parallel circuits*, you can switch off one light and others will stay on.

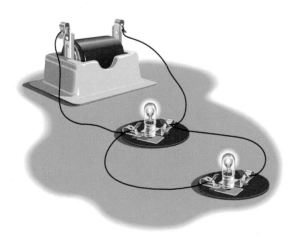

physical change (fiz′i kəl chānj) A change in size, shape, or state of matter in which no new matter is formed. (B48) Cutting an apple in half and freezing water into ice cubes are *physical changes*.

physical property (fiz′i kəl präp′ər tē) A characteristic of a material or object that can be seen or measured without changing the material into a new substance. (B12) One *physical property* of a ball is its round shape.

polar climate (pō′lər klī′mət) A very cold climate that does not receive much energy from the Sun. (E85) The Arctic has a *polar climate*.

pollutant (pə lo͞ot′′nt) A substance that causes pollution. (A65) The exhaust gases from cars add *pollutants* to the air.

pollution (pə lo͞o′shən) The dirtying of the environment with waste materials or other unwanted substances. (A65) Water *pollution* can cause disease or even death in living things.

precipitation (prē sip ə tā′shən) Any form of water that falls from clouds to Earth's surface. (E46) Rain, snow, and hail are forms of *precipitation*.

property (präp′ər tē) A characteristic that describes matter. (B12) Hardness is a *property* of steel.

R

rain gauge (rān gāj) A device for measuring precipitation. (E47) The *rain gauge* at the weather station showed that 2 cm of rain had fallen in 24 hours.

recycle (rē sī′kəl) To process and reuse materials. (A72) Discarded newspapers are *recycled* to make new paper.

relative humidity (rel′ə tiv hyo͞o mid′ə tē) The amount of water vapor present in the air at a given temperature compared to the maximum amount that the air could hold at that temperature. (E47) A *relative humidity* of 95 percent on a warm day can make you feel sticky and uncomfortable.

renewable resource (ri no͞o′ə-bəl rē′sôrs) A resource that can be replaced. (A42) Water is a *renewable resource* because rain increases the supply of water.

reptile (rep′təl) A vertebrate, such as a lizard or a crocodile, that has dry scaly skin and lays eggs that have a leathery shell. (C20) *Reptiles* can be found in both deserts and rain forests.

river system (riv′ər sis′təm) A river and all the waterways, such as brooks, streams, and rivers, that drain into it. (A11) The Mississippi River and the many waterways feeding into it make up the largest *river system* in the country.

rock (räk) A solid material that is made up of one or more minerals and that may be used for its properties. (A41) Granite is a hard *rock* used in construction.

S

sand dune (sand do͞on) A mound, hill, or ridge of sand formed by the wind. (A21) *Sand dunes* are common in the desert.

sand dune

savanna (sə van′ə) A broad, grassy plain that has few or no trees. (C48) Nearly half of Africa is covered by *savannas*.

sediment (sed′ə mənt) Sand, soil, and rock carried by water, wind, or ice. (A12) The rushing water of the river deposited *sediment* along the riverbanks.

seed plants (sēd plants) Plants that reproduce with seeds. (C35) Corn and wheat are *seed plants*.

series circuit (sir′ēz sur′kit) An electric circuit in which the parts are connected in a single path. (D50) Electric current can follow only one path in a *series circuit*.

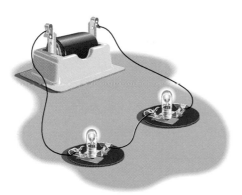

soil (soil) Loose material that covers much of Earth's land surface and is made up of three layers—topsoil, subsoil, and partly weathered rock. (A30) Plants, insects, and worms live in *soil*.

solar cell (sō′lər sel) A device that changes sunlight into electrical energy. (D64) *Solar cells* used in power plants can produce electricity without polluting the air.

solar energy (sō′lər en′ər jē) The clean and relatively low-cost energy from the Sun. (A50, D64) *Solar energy* is used to heat water in some homes.

solid (säl′id) Matter that has a definite volume and a definite shape. (B29) A *solid*, such as a rock, a wooden block, or an ice cube, has a definite volume and shape.

solution (sə lōō′shən) A mixture in which the particles of different substances are mixed evenly. (B51) Stirring sugar into water makes a *solution*.

Southern Hemisphere (su*th*′ərn hem′i sfir) The half of Earth south of the equator. (E79) The island continent Australia is in the *Southern Hemisphere*.

south pole (south pōl) One of the ends of a magnet where the magnetic force is strongest; it points to the south when the magnet moves freely. (D13) The *south pole* of one magnet attracts the north pole of another magnet.

standard unit (stan′dərd yōōn′it) A unit of measure that everyone agrees to use. (B19) Scientists use the gram as the *standard unit* of mass.

state of matter (stāt uv mat′ər) Any of the three forms that matter may ordinarily take: solid, liquid, and gas. (B29) When ice melts, it changes to a liquid *state of matter.*

static electricity (stat′ik ē lek-tris′i tē)) Electric charges that have built up on the surface of an object. (D31) Walking across a carpet on a cold, dry day can produce *static electricity.*

stratus cloud (strāt′əs kloud) A low, flat cloud that often brings drizzle. (E55) Large sheets of very dark *stratus clouds* covered the sky on the rainy morning.

substance (sub′stəns) A class of matter made up of elements and compounds. (B34) Salt and sugar are *substances.*

switch (swich) A device that completes or breaks the path a current can follow in an electric circuit. (D41) In order to turn on the light, you must press the *switch* to complete the circuit.

temperate climate (tem′pər it klī′mət) A climate that generally has warm, dry summers and cold, wet winters. (E85) Most regions of the United States have a *temperate climate.*

theory (thē′ə rē) A hypothesis that is supported by a lot of evidence and is widely accepted by scientists. (S9) The big-bang *theory* offers an explanation for the origin of the universe.

thunderstorm (thun′dər stôrm) A storm that produces lightning and thunder and often heavy rain and strong winds. (E66) When the weather is hazy, hot, and humid, *thunderstorms* are likely to develop.

tornado (tôr nā′dō) A violent, funnel-shaped storm of spinning wind. (E72) The wind speed at the center of a *tornado* can be twice that of hurricane winds.

tropical climate (träp′i kəl klī′mət) A hot, rainy climate. (E85) Areas that are near the equator have a *tropical climate* because they receive the greatest amount of energy from the Sun.

troposphere (trō′pō sfir) The layer of the atmosphere closest to the surface of Earth. (E12) The *troposphere* reaches about 11 km above the surface of Earth and is the layer of the atmosphere in which weather occurs.

variable (ver′ē ə bəl) The one difference in the setups of a controlled experiment; provides a comparison for testing a hypothesis. (S7) The *variable* in an experiment with plants was the amount of water given each plant.

vertebra (vʉr′tə brə) One of the bones that together make up the backbone. (C14) Each knob in your backbone is a *vertebra*.

vertebrate (vʉr′tə brit) An animal that has a backbone. (C14) Reptiles and birds are *vertebrates*.

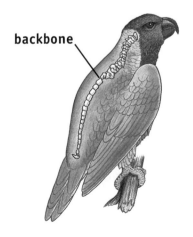

backbone

voltage (vōl′tij) The force of an electric current, measured in volts. (D63) Electric currents of high *voltage* travel through long-distance power lines.

volume (väl yo͞om) The amount of space that matter takes up. (B10) A baseball has a greater *volume* than a golf ball does.

warm front (wôrm frunt) The leading edge of a warm air mass that forms as the warm air mass moves forward into a cold air mass. (E63) Light rain often falls along a *warm front*.

water cycle (wôt′ər si′kəl) The movement of water into the air as water vapor and back to Earth's surface as rain, snow, or hail. (E46) The *water cycle* is powered by energy from the Sun.

water vapor (wôt′ər vā′pər) Water that is in the form of a gas. (E10) *Water vapor* from the air forms drops of water on cold glass surfaces.

weather (we*th*′ər) The condition of the atmosphere at a certain place and time. (E13) The *weather* today in Chicago is snowy.

weather forecaster (we*th*'ər fôr'kast ər) A person who makes weather predictions or reports weather conditions. (E61) The *weather forecaster* predicted rain for the next three days.

weather satellite (we*th*'ər sat''l īt) A human-made device in space that takes pictures of Earth and collects information about the weather. (E54) The *weather satellite* sent back pictures of clouds to weather stations in different locations on the ground.

weathering (we*th*'ər iŋ) The physical and chemical processes by which rock is broken down into smaller pieces. (A10) Cracks in rock produced by freezing rainwater or the growth of plant roots are examples of *weathering*.

wind (wind) The movement of air over Earth's surface. (E21) The strong *wind* lifted the kite high above the houses.

windsock (wind'säk) A device used to show wind direction, consisting of a cloth bag that is open at both ends and hung on a pole. (E38) The *windsock* showed that the wind was blowing from the north.

wind vane (wind vān) A device, often shaped like an arrow, used to show the direction of the wind. (E38) The *wind vane* on the roof of the weather station showed that the wind was blowing from the southwest.

INDEX

* Activity

* Activity

CREDITS

ILLUSTRATORS
Cover: Genine Smith.

Think Like a Scientist: 14: Laurie Hamilton. *Border:* Genine Smith.

Unit A: 11, 13: Susan Johnston Carlson. 13–15: Paul Mirocha. 22–24: Jim Turgeon. 23, 25: Skip Baker. 30–31: Brad Gaber. 32–33: Jim Salvati. 38–39: Dave Joly. 39: Eldon Doty. 40: Brad Gaber. 43: Terry Ravenelli. 44: Terry Boles. 46: Rodica Prato. 47: Martucci Studio. 51: Brad Gaber. 56: Jim Trusilo. 58–59: Robert Roper. 61: Ray Vella. 63: Michael Ingle. 64: Greg Harris. 65: Robert Roper. 68: Greg Harris. 69–71: Bob Ostrom. 71: Eldon Doty. 72–74: Scott MacNeil. 76: Ken Bowser. 77: Randy Chewning.

Unit B: 12–13: Nina Laden. 18: Dave Winter. 19: Terry Boles. 19–22: Mark Bender. 29–31: J.A.K. Graphics. 32: Susan Johnston Carlson. 33: Tom Buches. 34–35: J.A.K. Graphics. 38, 40–41: Ron Fleming. 43: J.A.K. Graphics. 49: Andrew Shiff. 53: Patrick Gnan. 59: Bob Doucet. 60: Dartmouth Publishing.

Unit C: 8–9: Lee Steadman. 12–13: Susan Melrath. 13: Linda Warner. 13: Eldon Doty. 14–15: Dave Barber. 18–20: Jim Deal. 30: Barbara Hoopes Ambler. 35: Wendy Smith-Griswold. 40–41: Phil Wilson. 44: Jackie Urbanovic. 44–47: Julie Tsuchya. 48–49: Linda Howard. 54–57: Richard Cowdrey. 59–60: Randy Hamblin.

Unit D: 13: Patrick Gnan. 15: Dan McGowan. 22: Brad Gaber. 30–31: Robert Roper. 35: *t.* Jim Effier; *m.* Andrew Shiff. 40: David Winter. 41: Hans & Cassady, Inc. 42–43: Dale Gustafson. 48: Patrick Gnan. 50–51: Hans & Cassady, Inc. 52: Robert Roper. 53: Hans & Cassady, Inc. 60–61: Robert Roper. 62–63: Geoffrey McCormick. 68–69: Vincent Wayne. 70, 72: Robert Roper. 74–76: Michael Sloan.

Unit E: 11, 13: Randy Hamblin. 14–15: Robert Roper. 20: Andy Lendway. 22: Flora Jew. 23: Robert Roper. 30: Susan Melrath. 31: Rob Burger. 32: Tom Pansini. 33: Rob Burger. 38–39: Pamela Becker. 46: Michael Kline. 49: Rob Burger. 55: Gary Torrisi. 56: Patrick Gnan. 60: Kristin Kest. 60: Thomas Cranmer. 61 63: Nancy Tobin. 62: Robert Roper. 66, 68–70: Tom Lochray. 71: Gary Torrisi. 72: Tom Lochray. 73: Gary Torrisi. 77: Josie Yee. 78: Mike Quon. 79: Josie Yee. 80–81: John Youssi. 84–85: Thomas Cranmer. 86–87: Uldis Klavins. 90–92: Julie Peterson. 93: John Youssi.

Math and Science Toolbox: *Logos:* Nancy Tobin. 14–15: Andrew Shiff. *Borders:* Genine Smith.

Glossary 17: *t.r.* Dan McGowan. *m.l.* Richard Cowdrey. *b.r.* Dale Gustafson. 18: Mike Quon. 19: Dale Gustafson. 20: Dan McGowan. 21,22: Dale Gustafson. 23: Robert Roper. 24: A.J. Miller. 26,27: Patrick Gnan. 28: Hans & Cassady Inc. 29: Dan McGowan. 30: Hans & Cassady Inc. 32: David Barber. 33: Patrick Gnan.

PHOTOGRAPHS
All photographs by Houghton Mifflin Co. (HMCo.) unless otherwise noted.

Front Cover: *t.* Superstock; *m.l.* Bill Brooks/Masterfile Corporation; *m.r.* Tim Flach/Tony Stone Images; *b.l.* Barbara Leslie/FPG International; *b.r.* Greg Ryan & Sally Beyer/Tony Stone Images.

Table of Contents iv: *l.* Harold Sund/The Image Bank; *r.* Cromosohm/Sohm/The Stock Market. viii: Stan Osolinski/The Stock Market. xiii: *t.r.* Brian Parker/Tom Stack & Associates; *b.l.* Tony Freeman/PhotoEdit; *b.m.* Buff Corsi/Tom Stack & Associates; *b.r.* Gary Withey/Bruce Coleman Incorporated. xiv: © 2000 Juha Jormanainen/Woodfin Camp & Associates. xv: *l.* NOAA; *r.* NOAA/NESDIS/NCDC/SDSD.

Think Like a Scientist: 2: *t. bkgd.* PhotoDisc, Inc. 3: *t.* PhotoDisc, Inc. 4–5: *bkgd.* Chip Henderson Photography.

Unit A 1: Kim Heacox/Tony Stone Images. 2–3: Kim Heacox/Tony Stone Images. 4: Mark Hopkins. 4–5: *bkgd.* Miriam Romais; *m.t.* Miriam Romais; *t.* Miriam Romais; *m.b.* Miriam Romais; *b.* Miriam Romais. 10: *l.* E.R. Degginger/Color-Pic, Inc.; *m.* C.C. Lockwood/DRK Photo; *r.* Cameron Davidson/Comstock. 12: *l.* Tom Stack & Associates; *r.* Manfred Gottschalk/Tom Stack & Associates. 13: Scott Blackman/Tom Stack & Associates. 14: *l.* E.R. Degginger/Color-Pic, Inc.; *r.* NASA/Corbis Media. 15: Bob Daemmrich Photography. 20–21: *bkgd.* Larry Ulrich/DRK Photo; *inset* Breck P. Kent Photography. 21: Breck P. Kent Photography. 22: *l.* E.R. Degginger/Color-

Pic, Inc.; *r.* Breck P. Kent Photography. 22–23: © Porterfield/Chickering/Photo Researchers, Inc. 24: Spencer Swanger/Tom Stack & Associates. 26–27: *bkgd.* Richard Hamilton Smith/Corbis Corporation; *inset* Thanh H. Dao/USDA-ARS-CPRL. 32: *t.* Harold Sund/The Image Bank; *b.* J.C. Carton/Bruce Coleman Incorporated. 33: *t.* Kevin Schafer/Tom Stack & Associates; *b.* John Callahan/Tony Stone Images. 34: Grant Huntington for HMCo. 36: Grant Huntington for HMCo. 36–37: Grant Huntington for HMCo. 37: Grant Huntington for HMCo. 41: Grant Huntington for HMCo. 43: *t.l.* Edward Bower/The Image Bank; *t.r.* Lester Lefkowitz/Tony Stone Images; *b.l.* Lester Lefkowitz/Tony Stone Images. 49: *t.l.* J. Barry O'Rourke/The Stock Market; *t.r.* J. Barry O'Rourke/The Stock Market; *b.* © Ludek Pesek/Photo Researchers, Inc.; *inset* Mike Abrahams/Tony Stone Images. 50: Cromosohm/Sohm/The Stock Market. 52–53: *bkgd.* Paul Conklin/PhotoEdit; *inset* Robert Holmgren Photography. 64: Frans Lanting/Minden Pictures. 66: Grant Heilman Photography, Inc. 67: *t.* Larry Lefever/Grant Heilman Photography, Inc.; *b.* Runk/Schoenberger/Grant Heilman Photography, Inc. 74: *l.* © Donald S. Heintzelman/Photo Researchers, Inc.; *r.* © Will McIntyre/Photo Researchers, Inc.

Unit B 1: © Vito Palmisano/Photo Researchers, Inc. 2–3: © Vito Palmisano/Photo Researchers, Inc. 4: Melvin Epps/Third Eye Production. 4–5: *bkgd.* Martina Johnson-Allen; *inset* Martina Johnson-Allen. 13: *t.r.* © Milton Heiberg/Photo Researchers, Inc.; *b.r.* David Young-Wolff/PhotoEdit. 24–25: *bkgd.* © Chris Marona/Photo Researchers, Inc.; *inset* Los Alamos National Laboratory. 26: Grant Huntington for HMCo. 27: Grant Huntington for HMCo. 28: *t.* Grant Huntington for HMCo.; *b.* Grant Huntington for HMCo. 29: *l.* Light Images, Inc.; *m.* Al Clayton/International Stock; *r.* Miwako Ikeda/International Stock. 34: Grant Huntington for HMCo. 36: Grant Huntington for HMCo. 37: Grant Huntington for HMCo. 39: Barry L. Runk/Grant Heilman Photgraphy, Inc. 42: *l.* Zefa Germany/The Stock Market; *m.* Greg Ryan & Sally Beyer/Positive Reflections; *r.* Richard Hutchings for HMCo. 46: Grant Huntington for HMCo. 47: Grant Huntington for HMCo. 48: Grant Huntington for HMCo. 48–49: Grant Huntington for HMCo. 50: *t.* Grant Huntington for HMCo.; *b.* Grant Huntington for HMCo. 51: *t.* © George Whitely/Photo Researchers, Inc. 52: Grant Huntington for HMCo. 54: Grant Huntington for HMCo. 55: *t.* Grant Huntington for HMCo.; *b.* Grant Huntington for HMCo. 56–57: John Gurzinski. 57: *l.* Superstock; *r.* Robert Brenner/PhotoEdit. 58: Jim Smalley/The Picture Cube. 59: Grant Huntington for HMCo. 61: *l.* Grant Huntington for HMCo.; *r.* Grant Huntington for HMCo.

Unit C 1: Stuart Westmorland/Tony Stone Images. 2–3: Stuart Westmorland/Tony Stone Images. 4–5: *bkgd.* Inga Spence/Tom Stack & Associates; *inset* Frans Lanting/Minden Pictures. 7: Richard Hutchings for HMCo. 10: *t.l.* © Tom McHugh/Photo Researchers, Inc.; *t.r.* Jane Burton/Bruce Coleman Incorporated; *b.* © Hermann Eisenbeiss/Photo Researchers, Inc. 11: *t.* Dwight R. Kuhn; *m.l.* © Michael Abbey/Photo Researchers, Inc.; *m.r.* © Gary Reterford/Science Source/Photo Researchers, Inc.; *b.l.* Kim Taylor/Bruce Coleman Incorporated; *b.r.* © Biophoto Associates/Science Source/Photo Researchers, Inc. 19: *t. to b.* Dwight R. Kuhn; Donald Specker/Animals Animals/Earth Scenes; E.R. Degginger/Color-Pic, Inc.; Zig Leszczynski/Animals Animals/Earth Scenes; Dwight R. Kuhn. 20: Art Wolfe/Tony Stone Images. 21: *bkgd.* David Sailors/The Stock Market; *l.* G.I. Bernard/Oxford Scientific Films/Animals Animals/Earth Scenes; *inset* Al Hamdan/The Image Bank. 22: *t.* Doug Perrine/DRK Photo; *b.* S. Nielsen/Imagery. 23: © Tom & Pat Leeson/Photo Researchers, Inc. 25: Richard Hutchings for HMCo. 26: *t.* Dwight R. Kuhn; *b.l.* The Granger Collection, New York; *b.r.* B.W. Payton. 27: *bkgd.* Larry Lipsky/Bruce Coleman Incorporated; *inset* M.C. Chamberlain/DRK Photo. 28: *t.* M.C. Chamberlain/DRK Photo; *b.l.* Mike Severns/Tom Stack & Associates; *b.r.* Brian Parker/Tom Stack & Associates. 29: *t.l.* Carl Roessler/Bruce Coleman Incorporated; *t.r.* Carol L. Geake/Animals Animals/Earth Scenes; *b.* Stephen Frink/Corbis Media. 31: *l. to r.* E.R. Degginger/Color-Pic, Inc.; James Cotier/Tony Stone Images; Andrew J. Martinez/Stock Boston; E.R. Degginger/Color-Pic, Inc.; Charles Sleicher/Tony Stone Images; Rosemary Calvert/Tony Stone Images. 32: *l.* © Rod Planck/Photo Researchers, Inc.; *r.* Phil Degginger/Color-Pic, Inc. 34: *t.l.* E.R. Degginger/Color-Pic, Inc.; *t.r.* © Alan & Linda Detrick/Photo Researchers, Inc.; *m.r.* Maximillian Stock/Stock Food America; *b.l.* Ray Pfortner/Peter Arnold, Inc.; *b.r.* E.R. Degginger/Color-Pic, Inc.; *l. inset* Tom & Pat Leeson/DRK Photo; *r. inset* E.R. Degginger/Color-Pic, Inc. 36: *t.l.* Runk/Schoenberger/Grant Heilman Photography, Inc.; *t.r.* © Alvin E. Staffan/Photo Researchers, Inc.; *b.l.* K.G. Preston Mafham/Animals Animals/Earth Scenes; *b.r.* Carl Wolinsky/Stock Boston. 37: *t.l.* © Dan Suzio/Photo Researchers, Inc.; *t.r.* © Dan Suzio/Photo Researchers, Inc. 38: *l.* E.R. Degginger/Color-Pic, Inc. 39: © Tom McHugh/Photo Researchers, Inc. 42: Stan Osolinski/The Stock Market. 43: *t.l.* © Renate & Gerd Wustig/Okapia/Photo Researchers, Inc.; *t.r.* Gary W. Griffen/Animals Animals/Earth Scenes; *b.l.* Robert A. Ross/Color-Pic, Inc.; *b.r.* Fred Bruemmer/DRK Photo. 44: *bkgd.* Spencer Swanger/Tom Stack & Associates; *inset* E.R. Degginger/Color-Pic, Inc. 45: *t.l.* Fred Fellerman/Tony Stone Images; *t.r.* Peter Drowne/Color-Pic, Inc.; *b.* Robert Maier/Animals Animals/Earth Scenes. 46: *t.* John Cancalosi/Tom Stack & Associates; *b.l.* R.J.B. Goodale/Animals Animals/Earth Scenes; *b.r.* M.C. Chamberlin/DRK Photo. 47: © Craig K. Lorenz/Photo Researchers, Inc. 54: *l.* © Cosmos Blank/National Audubon Society/Photo Researchers, Inc. 55: *l.* M. Austerman/Animals Animals/Earth Scenes; *r.* C.C. Lockwood/Animals Animals/Earth Scenes. 56: *t.* © M. Reardon/Photo Researchers, Inc.; *b.* Charlie Palek/Animals Animals/Earth Scenes. 57: *t.* Rod Planck/Tony Stone Images. 59: CNP/Archive Photos. 61: C.C. Lockwood/Animals Animals/Earth Scenes.

Unit D 1: Kennan Ward/The Stock Market. 2–3: Kennan Ward/The Stock Market. 4–5: *bkgd.* © Thomas Porett/Photo Researchers, Inc.; *inset* Grace Moore for HMCo. 6–7: Ken Karp for HMCo. 7: Ken Karp for HMCo. 10: Ken Karp for HMCo. 14: © 2000 Thomas Raupach/Woodfin Camp & Associates. 16: Ken Karp for HMCo. 17: Ken Karp for HMCo. 18: Ken Karp for HMCo. 23: *l.* E.R. Degginger/Color-Pic, Inc.; *r.* Science Exploratorium. 24: S. Nielsen/Imagery. 26–27: *bkgd.* Bob McKeever/Tom Stack & Associates; *inset* Billy Hustace. 27: © Dave